T0366651

Tricks of the Light

TRICKS OF THE LIGHT

New and Selected Poems

Vicki Hearne

Edited with an Introduction by John Hollander

The University of Chicago Press
Chicago & London

Vicki Hearne was born in 1946 in Austin, Texas. Celebrated as a poet and writer on the relations between domestic animals and humans, she was also a noted dog and horse trainer who was inducted posthumously into the International Association of Canine Professionals Hall of Fame in 2002. She died in 2001 in Branford, Connecticut.

John Hollander is Sterling Professor Emeritus of English at Yale University. The most recent of his many books of poetry is *Picture Window* (2003). He edited the Library of America's two-volume anthology, *Nineteenth-Century American Poetry* (1993), and is the author of *The Gazer's Spirit: Poems Speaking to Silent Works of Art* (1995), the latter published by the University of Chicago Press.

The University of Chicago Press, Chicago 60637
The University of Chicago Press, Ltd., London
© 2007 by The Estate of Vicki Hearne
All rights reserved. Published 2007
Printed in the United States of America

16 15 14 13 12 11 10 09 08 07   1 2 3 4 5

ISBN-13: 978-0-226-32241-4 (cloth)
ISBN-10: 0-226-32241-6 (cloth)

Library of Congress Cataloging-in-Publication Data

Hearne, Vicki, 1946–
    Tricks of the light : new and selected poems / Vicki Hearne ; edited by John Hollander.
        p.   cm.
    Includes bibliographical references and index.
    ISBN-13: 978-0-226-32241-4 (cloth : alk. paper)
    ISBN-10: 0-226-32241-6 (cloth : alk. paper)
    I. Hollander, John. II. Title.
    PS3558.E2555T75   2007
    811'.54—dc22
2006033044

❧ Contents ❧

Tricks of the Light

from *Nervous Horses* (1980)

꙳

from *In the Absence of Horses* (1983)

✤

from *The Parts of Light* (1994)

Publisher's Note

Although the author intended to dedicate this book to John Hollander and began to draft words to accompany the final version of the manuscript, neither the author's literary executor nor the volume editor found what could safely be considered a final version of the dedicatory language. Since only the author could choose words that would convey what she wished Hollander to know, let this note serve in the place of that intent.

❦ Acknowledgments ❧

Grateful acknowledgment is made to the periodicals listed below where the poems from the "Posthumous Poems" section, or versions thereof, first appeared:

The American Scholar: "What Philosopher"

Denver Quarterly: "Painting Over Candles," "Hounds," "Going to Ground," "Dark Stars," "Decorum of Time," and "Delight in a Seasonal Shift" (As "Syntax: Its Seasonal Shift")

The Georgia Review: "Trained Man and Dog," vol. 58, no. 2 (Summer 2004)

The Hudson Review: "The Tree That Plucks Fruit"

Literary Imagination: "Heartdust: New Ride in Old Arroyo" and "Plato's Seventh Letter" reprinted from vol. 7, no. 1. Copyright 2005. Used by permission of The Association of Literary Scholars and Critics

Michigan Quarterly Review: "Getting It Right" and "Blinded by Glory"

New England Review: "Road to Beauty" and "Young Dog, Grass, and More" first published in vol. 25, no. 3

The Paris Review: "The Wax Figure Ruined"

Poetry: "January 6" first published in April 2004 (vol. 184, no. 1)

Raritan: "Clown on Tight Rope," "Opposite the Heart," "So There Is Justice," and "News from the Dogs"

Southwest Review: "A Subtle Gesture" appeared in vol. 89, no. 2 & 3, 2004

TriQuarterly: "Creatures of the Surface," "The Old Dog," "Wind Rubs Into," "White Out," "Without Mountains," and "Side View (Alumna Report)" first published in January 2006

Yale Review: "A World of Differences" and "Every Time the Mountains" first published in October 2004 (vol. 92, no. 4)

❧ Introduction ❧

Vicki Hearne, well known for her remarkable essays on the relation of humans to domestic animals—some of them published in *Adam's Task,* and *Animal Happiness*—was a poet of extraordinary gifts and surprising resources. One of the more unusual aspects of her talent is manifested in the way her poetry reflects just how her whole working and thinking life defeats clichés of expectation. A professional trainer of both dogs and horses, she wrote in a way that was always vibrant with direct knowledge of animals wild and tame. But she was also a philosophically oriented thinker concerned with such matters as the "private language" argument in Wittgenstein's *Philosophical Investigations,* or the mythography of Plato's fable of horse and rider, or the ethical implications of Renaissance training manuals, or the folklore of modern handlers, and with how these matters themselves can fall like shadows over actual animals, modeling rather than darkening them.

Her concerns were as theoretical as they were practical. She was a poet of true originality; her poems were intense, passionate, and drenched in thought, engaging major moral and epistemological concerns. She never wrote what is so common in mediocre poetry today: short pieces of exposition or anecdote in rather arbitrarily constructed verse. Rather she explored in late-modern lyrics the boundaries of their own figuration. In her poems "of" horses—and, later, dogs—she was never a sentimental anecdotalist or an editorializer. Instead, Hearne rejoiced in what might be called the Art of Domestication—not merely in the sense of a craft of training, but in the larger, related sense of the way in which the engagement of an unspeaking animal with the constructions of human language and thought is, in itself, a high aesthetic occasion.

Despite her reputation as a dog trainer with unpredictable views, her somewhat iconoclastic speculations in prose, and her store of knowledge of past and present modes of human dealings with domestic animals, Hearne's poetry can give no comfort to the sentimentalizers of the relation between the human Self and the animal Other, nor to sensationalists of expressiveness. The poems give no comfort to Humane Societies, nor, indeed, to other literalists, for her vast respect for the power and dignity of representation itself causes Hearne to release her animal subjects and their human agents out onto fields of metaphor far richer and more varied in their vegetation and contours than the narrow places of mere emblem.

Aware of the traditional philosophical problems of knowing other minds—of how, and even what, we know (and can't know) of others' thoughts and feelings—she writes from a variety of engagements with the simultaneously distant and intimate otherness of domestic animals and of their consciousness. This last, a beautifully hypothetical entity (both, as Wordsworth put it, what we half-create and perceive) that keeps flickering in and out of interest the more we know and are with them, comes up in much of her work, with the pointedness of argument in her prose, but obliquely pointed in her poems. Hearne's poems form a kind of romance in which our worries about how we ought sensibly to talk, and what the skilled experience of training animals leads one to feel and intuitively to say, are engaged in a dialectical sparring-match. In a way, her poems—whatever their palpable "subjects" or rhetorical stances—are often like training exercises for her own language as she brings it to bear on the problems emerging from her own serious contemplation of the everyday and the extraordinary.

Hearne is always attentive to the matter of *mimesis*—of representation, so that human language and interpretable animal responses to human communication are part of a natural continuum. Her particular poetic world is one framed by a sensitivity to and concern for the mutual inter-representation of people and domestic animals. And since it is indeed a poetic world, each of the two is capable of being seen as metaphoric of the other. Her feeling for the nuanced power of representativeness confronts the making of sculpture (as in some of her last poems), or philosophical arguments, or other representations, ranging from fictions of the heart and mind to painted images. The poems in her first book, *Nervous Horses* (1980), largely in supple, modulated, and beautifully controlled syllabic verse, were neither mock training-manuals nor the journal-notes of a self-conscious rider. Rather, they often puzzle and are puzzled themselves. The horses of her title are both sinewy and agitated, as they are both actual and figurative: they are the horses of modernity, and are made up of knowledge and observation of both poetry and animals. In a poem called "Genuine and Poignant" (not included in this volume), Hearne shows that she has learned well Wallace Stevens's first lessons in poetic dressage:

> Just that once, not to grieve, and the hill
> To stand suddenly bare and pure
> Confidently shaking its dust through the warm window.

But she moves in other poems to the more animated subject of her horses and, subsequently, to her dogs. She treats the otherness of animals as intimate and terrifying. The hypothetical consciousness of these animals is among the realms that this first collection so wonderfully explores.

From the outset, Hearne appears to be particularly concerned to avoid the way in which so much contemporary verse sets up and relates crude concepts of subject and object, experience and image, in an unacknowledged and unexplored realm of thought. The final poem in *Nervous Horses*, "The Metaphysical Horse," is a fine meditation on coming to terms with one's own metaphors—in that particular case, conceptions are like mirror-images, but which, having been lived with and worked through, allowed her to end like this:

> Circling elegantly we
> Glimpse the always receding
> True proposal in the glass
>
> And join the horses, who dance,
> Tremors of exactitude
> Flaming, still fresh on their limbs.

Hearne's practical experience of horses is at one not only with her interest in their mythologies, but also with her work as a trainer of the elements of discourse. For a poet, language has a kind of life of its own, and the complex "exactitude," both of precision and of elicited exertion, resonates in the concerns of work, art, and moral imagination. Hearne herself has what she calls in the title of one poem "The Fastidiousness of the Musician." Exercise lessons, set problems, and puzzles are often her occasions. The longest poem from *Nervous Horses*, the penultimate "St. George and the Dragon," has a quasi-narrative line, and yet it records the quest not of the mounted knight but rather of the poet's for him, in the fragmentations of a jigsaw puzzle. The problem (signaled in the subtitle of the poem) of piecing together an imaginative construction that will hold harks back to James Merrill's jigsaw puzzle of memory in his crucial "Lost in Translation." Hearne's poem modulates this into an amusingly domesticated metaphor in which friends and teachers help the poet cope with the epistemological problems, trials, and errors that occupy the whole of this distinguished first book.

Nervous Horses was followed by a more remarkable second book, full of poems capable of both greater rhetorical ease and more complex philosophical meditation, the work of an ear even more finely tuned and a mind more subtly and powerfully engaged. *In the Absence of Horses* (1983) avowed in its title the kind of metaphorical transcendent revision, or transumption (as some rhetoricians call it), of a previous agenda that is always, for true art, a necessity like breathing. Much of the poetry in this second volume interprets the title to emphasize that tropes are tropes, and that poetic meditation is not the recital of technical commonplaces. A poem called "Our Condition at Twilight" makes clear what remains of some of the Imagination's tasks and predicaments. We see this, too, in an ecphrastic poem, titled "Gauguin's White Horse," wherein taking the act of painting as seriously as she does—not acting like a reductive practical trainer and muttering something about how the horse couldn't be standing in that position . . . etc.—were somehow doing honor to the relations between horses and people; so that,

> . . . We with our
>
> Breathing as heavy, as rapid
> As paint, reach to pluck the horse,
> Letting time back in, and take
>
> Flesh for the trope of the horse,
> The horse for a trope of grace,
> Perception in place of the
>
> Acts of the heart, for granted . . .

And the fine title sequence introduces manifest questions of love into her pool of poetic reflections. By the end of it, in the final, ninth poem of the sequence, Hearne can make this plain, even as she now subtly—but swervingly—echoes Stevens's "Of Modern Poetry":

> Our study is poetry,
> Is the art of the horseman
> In whose gaze the world dances,
> The art of the mind finding
> The heart turning in the press
> Of the mind. The horse enters
> The turn of the heart. The heart
> Enters the turn of the poem . . .

It was, finally, in her very powerful third book, *The Parts of Light* (1994), that the absence of horses began to be refigured by means of the presence of dogs in many of the poems toward the end of the volume, although quite a few others remain concerned with equestrian matters. It also contains a very fine consideration of Roger Van der Weyden's depiction of St. Luke painting the Virgin and—as she wrote later of both the painting and her own poem—the hazards it meditates on, of "being dangerously entranced by divine light." The very beautiful title poem from this third collection introduces an allegory of light that plays over all her subsequent work, and which is most evident in the poetry she herself selected for publication in this new and selected volume.

The thirty-six posthumous poems (including the long, shockingly original five-part title sequence, "Tricks of the Light") explore some of her previously traveled terrain, but with a greater concern for its edges and deceptive contours. The weather, the activity of painting and sculpting, arguments with Plato, a continuing discourse with and of dogs, and always in these poems the array of different kinds of light—different figurations of it, but all somehow heading toward governing tropes of consciousness itself and, ultimately, language. This can be seen even in some of the more casually beautiful short poems like "White Out," "Getting It Right," and "Every Time the Mountain," and in parts of the long poem itself. Running to something like 360 lines in five numbered sections, the sequence starts out with the image of a young girl "hot with light" riding a stallion (returned to briefly later on in the poem) and subsequently moves through its heavily enjambed free-verse tercets with an almost Pindaric profusion of images in complex periodic sentences that, in the course of the poem, seem to be representing rhythms of thought rather than that of archaic eloquence, making of qualification and revision a matter of advance rather than of backtracking. So, for example, this passage from Part IV:

> . . . Why the bureaucrat
>
> cannot know the dog with stars
> caught up in her teeth
> like a song, is a question
>
> for the bureaucrat or else
> the high giggling moon,
> shamed when an idea leaps

across a shadow, making noon
cavort among the oak leaves
until proof comes round at last

to merge with the leap, no,
confess a history of leaping,
become one with the steadiness

of the sheepdog's eye as the promise
of language flickers
at the edge of vision.

This whole beautiful and difficult poem moves from lyric meditation to ana-lytic questionings to anecdotal and exemplary glimpses of particular dogs, for example these three who appear in the poem shortly after the passage just quoted:

Curry's style is solid
as she snaps up the dumbbell
as if it were an idea . . .

. . . Quincy
takes one stride in four

when the spirit is in him,
more and more often
in the golden weather.

Chili tumbles
to the idea of work,
caught up for the nonce

in the reality
that defies moral theory,
though he will slip again.

A strong, sad poem from Hearne's last published volume called "All of My Beautiful Dogs Are Dying," ends with the following lines, which, as I have observed elsewhere, make for what might seem to be a palinode—a poetic set-piece of retraction or recantation—but which was, in fact, a kind of affirmation:

. . . Without the beautiful dogs
No one dares to attend to desire;

The sky retreats, will intend nothing,
It is a ceiling to rebuke the gaze,
Mock the poetry of knowledge.

My death is my last acquiescence;
Theirs is the sky's renunciation,
Proof that the world is a scattered shame

Littering the heavens. The new dogs
Start to arise, but the sky must go
Deeply dark before the stars appear.

This seems sadly prophetic, of course; but it frames a central moment of vision for Hearne, emerging in the intellectual—and what some might want to call the spiritual—clarity that deep and knowledgeable love of darkness can afford.

Victoria Elizabeth Hearne was born in Austin, Texas, in 1946, grew up in that state, and, later, in California. She took a B.A. (1969) at the University of California at Riverside, majoring in English, and spent a good many years as a trainer of horses and dogs. Writing poetry during this time as well, she received a Stegner Fellowship at Stanford University, where she studied with the poet and critic Donald Davie in 1976–77. She had already published two books of poems when her important and celebrated prose work, *Adam's Task: Calling Animals by Name,* appeared in 1986. It was for this book, as well as for her poetry, that the American Academy of Arts and Letters, in giving her one of their awards in literature, cited her as writing "in a unique and powerful way of the relations between people and animals, and with a special regard for the rights of the imagination, and for the connections between work and love."

Hearne had taught in the creative writing program at the University of California, Riverside (1981–84), then later moved to Westbrook, Connecticut, with her second husband, Robert Tragesser, and taught in the Department of English at Yale University from 1984 to 1986, after which she remained a Visiting Fellow of Yale's Institute for Social and Policy Studies from 1989 to 1995. Her daughter, Colleen Mendelsohn, is a veterinarian living in California. Aside from Hearne's three books of poetry, Hearne's prose works also include the novel *The White German Shepherd* (1988), *Bandit: Dossier of a Dangerous Dog* (1991), and *Animal Happiness* (1994). She died in Connecticut in August of 2001.

I first got to know Vicki Hearne some time before I was even aware that she wrote poetry. She had written me about a possible reading in California more than thirty years ago, and we continued corresponding about matters of poetry thereafter. I only came to meet her on a visit to the University of California at Riverside a few years later. When I asked her what it was she worked at, she replied that she trained dogs and horses, to which I may have responded in a less than fascinated way. But within a very few minutes she had elicited my complete absorption. She spoke right away of her interest in the relation between psychologists' behavioristic accounts of what an animal was doing when it was learning to respond to a command or signal, and the very different kinds of stories that trainers would tell each other—and themselves—about what was going on. When she began to meditate on why it was that believing those stories helped the trainers work immeasurably better, I hesitantly mentioned that more general concerns of just that nature had been of interest to twentieth-century philosophers.

Before I could finish she was discussing particular passages of Wittgenstein's *Philosophical Investigations,* followed by her consideration of the history of observations on horse-training from Xenophon on through some Renaissance humanists. This was followed by all sorts of other historical accounts of such matters as the relation between humane societies and Tory politics in England, the cultural construction of breeds, together with such exemplary stories as that of the demonization of the Dobermann in the later 1930's as a Nazi dog, and a host of other tales, issues, problems, questions, and enigmas.

It was a good many months after this meeting and some subsequent correspondence that she sent me a few poems to read, being too intelligent and mannerly to have thrust them upon me at the time. I found them most authoritative in their strongly controlled diction and their lyrical adaptation of the rhythms of thought. Unusually impressive, too, was the way they framed those profound connections between form and fable that all true poetry must exhibit.

Over the next few years, her work began to show how much she had learned from that wonderful poet, critic, and teacher Donald Davie at Stanford. But it also continued to speak of the passionate knowledge and wonder of The Compleat Trainer (as I have thought of her), to whom I had listened with such fascination, and whose expertise in the training of animals and philosophical concerns for the epistemologies and moral overtones born of its theory and practice, would thereafter continue to inform—rather than crudely shape—her work. She was a distinguished member of a poetic generation in North America that included Debora Greger, Anne Carson, J. D. McClatchy, Louise Glück, John Koethe, Rachel Hadas, Alfred Corn, Marilyn Hacker, and A. F. Moritz (to name some of those who, for me, speak both to the intellect and the sensibility of their readership); it was also, in my experience, the first such poetic generation (all born within three or four years of Hearne) that numbered as many equally strong, thoughtful female poets as male (as has indeed remained the case since).

During the final months of her life, Vicki Hearne, in conjunction with the University of Chicago Press, was working on a volume of new and selected poetry, including the long, still unpublished poem "Tricks of the Light." The book you now have in hand, then, contains the author's own selections from her three published books, in addition to a considerable number of poems unpublished in any form at the time of her passing. In the weeks before her death, she sent the final manuscript of the book to the editor who secured periodical publication of most of the unpublished poems. The editor subsequently consulted with professors Susan Stewart and Colin (Joan) Dayan, collating it with earlier drafts of the selection. The present text departs from the author's manuscript only in placing the long poem at the end of the section of previously unpublished ones, and in some typographical corrections of erratic punctuation, spacing, capitalization, etc. In some instances, changes are recorded in the endnotes in this volume. To the rare occasional glossorial footnotes that Hearne provided, I have added a few notes of my own.

John Hollander, Woodbridge, Connecticut
July 2006

It has been our habit in the west, ever faithful to Homer, to elide certain figures. We give horses, sometimes winged, in the place of, or bearing the meaning of, the god, the hero, the lover, the poet, the knight of chastity, and any woman or any man when they are composed all of the chatter of gems.

But we can outlive, and out write, the ability to ride exalted horses.

Still, few, if they make the effort, outlive or out write the ability to send a good, or—if the gods should so will, a great—dog out into the fields of the imagination, and its forests, its planets.

I have put the supernatural—that is to say, great—dog in the place of the winged horse, as Homer did, and the good dogs in the place of the serviceable word.

Posthumous Poems

Creatures of the Surface

The dog may be a blue tick
Coonhound staunch against lamplight,

And mahogany Irish
Gayer than the singing strings,

A terrier, any breed,
Reaching into the darkness

With her teeth, thus, naming it
The enemy. A sheep dog,

All made of eye and angles
On the flock. For all we know

A lapdog, free style winner,
Or steady on a man trail.

Always a messenger true
To the world, to us giving

Up the task of the fulcrum
Or lore. We are not ourselves

To know. We are not to name
Any but the exoteric

Creatures of the surfaces.
We are to become pristine.

A tribal song of knowledge
Is the fate that, evaded,

Takes us to the depths, down to
The far and remote regions

Of logic which still demands
That the dog be *this* or *this*

Instead of variously
Emerging into the fields

Of learning as *this* and *this*.
This, and this, and also that

Floatable variation
Of heart, coming home to leave,

Leaving home to come
Sustaining a merriment

As of a polished fulcrum
Of leg-flash, on which our minds

For bare sustenance depend,
The young Airedale's head tosses

The light and catches it up
On his teeth; laughter's lesson

In the singularity
Of the plural, the many

Birds that on a single wing
Beat their way unwavering.

Knowledge opened. It closes,
Now, on the Old Family.

Other exemplaries of truth.
The nations kick them aside

As is the wont of nations
Greedy to hear a verdict.

Gods do not choose refusal
As an ardent tool fit for

Discrimination. They wait,
They welcome the dogs humbly

Like crumbs poor servants snatch up,
Like worlds wealthy dogs invent.

✤ A World of Differences

There are no dogs. Instead there exist
This that and the other bright angle
Of gaze on sheep, ways our invented

Bull pups are so quiet from brave hearts
That invent awareness—thus: Again
Each instant stutters into its song

Of all futures made possible. Why

Else do you think we have names and call
Them out numberless (not infinite)
Times, our own and others and the names

Of piebald ponies stark with hunger
Seen in all manner of smudged tractates
Published by liars? And the real world

As well, once in a while. What it is
About minds—the heedless young Airedale
The poet lost in a salt marsh once

He knew what loss was, the starving mind
Of the mindless punk, the full mind not
Distinguishable from the full heart

Of the scholar—is that none of them
Can be known and none of them can be
Without names for us. We are like this

Too, for every time we can answer
A new voice calling a name it brings
Us worlds of differences as if

Calling and responding were knowledge,
Knowing were living, as if the gaze
Of this eighteen-month-old Labrador

Bright with discovery, like
Spring's first squirrel named love
Quickening, while terror fails.

❧ Heartdust: New Ride in Old Arroyo

Our horses' hooves now reach down
The slope with us carefully,
Quickly, counting up the years

That slipped through the dry gullies
Since there was last an angel
For each of us, animals

Also, and praise in heaven.
In each peaceful arroyo
The idea of praise sifts

Gold through the dust; meaningful
Gleams organize new landscapes
Of the heart. The restless cats,

Stirring up heartdust as they
Pad gently after their prey,
Will do until new angels

Answer the respirations
Of the earth. What of wholeness
Emerges now is our own.

The air turns aside like air
For the great silky shoulders
Of our horses, who continue

As though their hooves were held up
By angels, the real become
Clean straw, deep grain, easy breath.

This desert's eternity
Is not comfort. It enfolds
Us in formal clarity,

Lengthens the lines of my horse
Whose legs become clean and long
In the light and in shadow

Making parallels; Euclid
Becomes a recent angel,
Meets us where light and shadow

And eternity are real.
This is as we expected:
We are taken by surprise.

Some Exactitudes of Wonder from an Old Quest Manual

for Robert, January 1, 1999

It is more usual to begin
With rubble, but fog,
As coy as light in a silk caftan,

Will serve. For the longest time it is,
Like any version of light, the most
Fraught with peril. You will find it

At its best in landscapes so thickened
With beauty that horses are required
To make sense of them and there, as you see,

Is why we have almost always had horses.
After Greek horses there are Greek hounds:
For light their paws, even along that true

Blue the sky finally gave up to
The painters, gave the word glitter,
Wrapped in love, to Ulysses, who saw

By that light what the fog takes away
Even from Argos. In any case,
Choose fog or rubble, whichever

Comes first. Change your horses
In mid stream. Just don't see any more
Than is really there. Or any less.

You will know you have chosen for once
And for all when suddenly the path
Shatters, kindling splintered dry with love

As the stars begin to soar, startled
Into their courses and far enough
Away from pure light for human eyes

To make them out. Now that there are stars
You know that you are on a quest.
Not far from home, (Forget about home.)

The material here to work with:
It's not fog and it is not rubble
And it is not that it is not fog

Or rubble. It is not even that
It is not of you, but that it is
Yours, given the way family is,

By logic. The book to be written
Will be as discrete as ever books
Of this sort are; you cannot lay it

Out plain in broad daylight any more
Than you can lay out the sprawled figures
Of the constellations of justice

At noon; this is why the questing beast
Waits until dark, must wait until dark
To lead you from the one perfect

Midnight to the next one. The cup waits.
The patience of the chalice is missed
By many earlier guides as the

Plain fact it is of our belonging
To it, our being born to inscribe
Ourselves in thirteen noble metals

At one stroke. Meanwhile you are in the fog
Or you have turned both your ankles.
On the rubble. Each droplet of fog

Has a name. Each shard of rubble is
Your only golden opportunity
To take measure. So take your measure.

The beast with the musics of the hounds
In her belly even now awaits
Your call. She is the one who recalls

Where your own heartbeats are secreted.
In these precisions, happiness
Is the only rational response.

Clown on Tight Rope

(given with a silver figurine)

I have an ineradicable
smile and the most
cheerful belly in creation.

The long bar I carry before me
like a gift for a god
of uncertain temper

is essential. Think of
how mathematics would fall
without equations. I have

a pigeon at each end
as gay as sterling
for that balance

that depends upon homage
to the center and homage
to the broad banks of night

beneath the rope. If I fall
I will break. My rope can shatter
if silver can and that way deny

the gleam of my feet. The birds of peace,
nurturing cooers,
cannot vie at all against

the orchestra. One bird's wings
are softly raised, the better
to cling to the light.

They and I are not real,
but the wreckage should we break
will be actual.

My silver suit, red
dots for legibility
does not belie my craft.

What reaches the audience
is silence in their hearts
then the drum roll.

Because I am silver I carry
you and the lights and the birds
in my eyes, and when my eyes

shake asunder the visions of what
I see will be real. You, too.
That rope ladder

leads to the source. Your costume
will fit, your belly grow cheerful,
while your heart suspends you like a bridge,

or like, at the eleventh hour,
help for the maiden as
suspension becomes the truth

as my clowning reveals
what you share with me, demanding
the lift of angels

as they desert us.

        NOW: the welcome home gasp
of recognition the crowd gives
when they see the clown's street clothes

as dusty as rust from neglect. As your own.
That gasp caps the act
and STILL with these hijinks

before them the audience believes in
every word and every muteness,
throwing their sheets of relief

under the clown, just before he falls
with nothing to say the way
the sage and the bard do.

Watch and listen: the aesthetics
of the pratfall govern you
while the sage and the bard show how

a precious metal spins out
the tale and corners
the truth for itself.

Getting It Right

Precise pressure on the bones
clears the breathing. It takes

the acutest and ablest
of friends, lovers or trainers

to get it right. The dog's eyes
can be commanded by touch

as by any other sense
of the real, philosophy

of the greenest of castles
of the mind notwithstanding.

Notwithstanding the silver
glow by which we later mark

the paths of horses who fly
beyond the thinnest of airs.

Here, wings are no help. It is
the pure turn away from turns

of earlier maps that guide
with the rarest nourishment

for the rarest breaths, delight
akin to pain and nothing

to take back *pour souvenir,*
nothing even of love but

a memory, transumed as
if by the harshest cradle

of a rock, clear light of a
subtle pressure on the bones.

✺ January 6

We must stop bragging. There are limits
For us to the cold and the twelfth night

Marks them all. Just off the coast of Maine
The lobster boats pass, dragging their nets.

Capsize once in a while, in water
Like that you die, that's all, that water

Isn't even frozen. Not even
Frozen, and that's as cold as it gets.

The hearts of birds beat voraciously
So they keep warm, so if you put out

A feeder, keep it full of the seeds
Their hearts feed on, then it is only

When their food runs out that you find them
Inexpressibly taut in hollows,

And that's as cold as it ever gets.

✌ Plato's Seventh Letter

Plato's objection to words:
They were unalterable.

To names: they were unstable,
lighting now on the straightness,

now on the roundness; his world
would never stop revolving,

and no taste for butterflies
was there for him, to sweeten

the case. The bitterest truth
was the one he refused first

and last. It confounds us now,
that words do not sway the waves

or persuade the wayward wind
yet no sailor reaches port

who does not speak up into
the wind; we are deserted

already and forever
by the butterfly's light craft

the elephant's ponderous one.
Word for word, we live with poems,

Or, word for word, without them.

🌿 The Old Dog

The old dog
would, as a puppy

would, grab truth, gladding the air.
There were leaps

that brought the trees to their height
death to its knees. She

lost no time, had nothing

to make up for. Now time
has lost itself

for her and God
did not consult me, God

moved in on her
with assault, with intent.

She is limp, there
is no further motive in her.

This love
leaves an iridescent tracery

behind, a veneer that keeps
the distance between me

and the world merely a thing.

The Novice Sculptor

Learns that we are, yes, responsible
For what we see in the clouds, not free
For more obdurate matter. The beasts
Have feelings too, and from our feelings
We bounce our interpretations up
To the clouds, but this does little harm
So long as there are shapings steady
As though there were mastery, as in
The clay there is, as in the wax there
Is the possibility of bronze:

Something announced out loud, not dreamed up
In idleness. Your grasp of miseries
In the clouds, pleasantries too, let go,
Relax, for the soul's truer labors
Begin where the clouds give themselves up,
Not to the old interpretation
Racket, but to the reality
Of what desire merely harbingers
Feebly, as a child's cry announces
The grandeurs of heritage the state
Will harden into. The tongue of the clouds
Is confounded, there is vanity
Rank in all of our dreams.

Opposite the Heart

And just opposite the heart
Sit the rising magistrates

In judgment. Judgment tainted
By the insufficiencies

Of summer torn wide open
By the cries of bees, winter

Closed by their silence. The tongue
Of a babbling hound the heart

Discounts however hot pressed
The fox. Opposite the heart

The babbler keeps court; someone
Must hear out the babbler

When God and the mind disdain
The futile news. The sleek dogs

Hear the babble as babble,
Laugh as the light of pity

Fattens on the elegance
Their careless strides still fling out

Like the seeds of gaiety
Into the air of malice.

When your good hound goes missing,
Something he knew may be what

Holds him to earth at the death,
While the fox frolics, fabled

For taking the sporting view
Of destruction; this is not

Domesticity; the fox
Is swift and sly; the ashes

Of the hounds the fox outran
Curl in the (call it) spring

Air and will do to remind
Us of the hound as well as

What of Alexandria
Remains in educated

Fugues without darkness. The pup
Who springs in the light not like

Joy but in joy knows nothing
Of nothingness. Once again

I emerge, with her, and if
Carefully, a little stiff, still

Match my stride to ignorance.
Above, way above, the Lion

Rules the heart. Her opposite
On earth is justice, marriage

Her compromise. Unearthlike,
In the heavens, the opposite

Star, the water bearer, pours
Untidy, chilly knowledge

Out like a beneficence,
Angelic words intersect

The path to the void, the path,
Too, to seasons without turn.

❧ Painting Over Candles

In a convent on a hill
near a holy city

a painting over candles
black with devotion

the smoke of devotion over
a gay declaration

mysterious impudence
god

not to demonstrate
too clearly

the matter
of the face

white will do too—
obscure the gold

gather the fire tightly
into ashes woe

the firmamentician
who believes

and the one
who doubts

the visible
invisible except

to the wandering eye
for the sake of which

it comes in through the window

❧ Wind Rubs Into

Wind rubs into the surfaces
of thorough waters, of sandstone

complete as hope. Wind rubs
against the grain of your life

like hope, wind scares up
the darkness which, left behind,
collects in the corners of knowledge,

nourishes the bright skitter
of those shyer creatures

who dash away with
nearly enough light

from time's skirts. This slows
the roll of seasons

into unknowable ease. Here is how we learn
name after name

for the unpronounceable light,
whose vice is violence

for the unpronounced
darkness whose vice is peace.

Light and dark, a cross-grained clerk,
bureaucrat at the pearly gates with

a boss. Technophobic, skeptical,
the boss's voice follows

his stomach
into Rome where a single season

brought out the wind, heir
to everything we love.

Imperfection is the toy
of the wind, its vice

and virtue the aroma
of movement, and

don't you cuss that fiddle boy
unless you want that fiddle out of tune.

Every Time the Mountains

Every time the mountains gather
In like this a brand new painter
Mentions something, as if modestly.

A group of horses swinging their necks
Resonate too, until the brightest
Of the pities dims them, the latest

Foal agrees to ordure, grabs at rest,
Reimbursed by rumors that confuse
Their kind with kindness. Soon the mountains

Frown and lean over us; the frightened
Horses forget the veracities
Of the *haute école,* plundered of trust.

All of us love unforgivably,
Each time, too, the mountains gather
So expressively. Unless we ask

The horses how they think of mountains,
How they live for beauty, how we do,
Knowledge is qualified, limited

As theirs is in the shy glare of love.

❧ Blinded by Glory

Blinded by glory
we measure the thickness

of light by
a reckoning long ago

outdated. Our skins
rebuke the attempt

to see forever
because to see

how the good young hound
grows secretly

in her sleep moving
by bounds

into the maw
of the world

is to desire light
more

than the hounds
desire trails.

Hence trinkets
of sky and hide

content the painter.
The one who knows

what lies like silk
in the dark.

❧ White Out

When the snow busily chews
At the edges of the light,
Catching the eyes up in lace

As in memory, the same old
Glint stings the bones each time, but
We admire the distinctions,

Say each one is different,
As though difference were not
The crash of meaning and no

Clarity such as pilots
Wait for, who fly up solo
At times as though time were the

Presence of love, not its drift.
As though snow were a lazy,
Unambitious appetite.

In certain storms each snowflake
Is a heart of light, lonesome
For our glow stilly hoarded

Against such luminous greed.
We are not pilots alone
In the storm. The light is ours.

✣ Without Mountains

In a land without mountains
there are no knowing learners. Sabbath
becomes a day of hiding, the air
loses its canniness, breath
closes, guarding the nature of divinity
from god.
    The mechanics of light
replace light in the sun's refusal
to choose one or the other, showing all
for nothing. Day and night replace
the chiaroscuro of thought and song
splutters out letters to the editor.

Beside me the lean and gracious regard
on my face of a dog reopens the breeze
in which the whisper of mountains begins
to gather. On this new kind
of air, new kinds of life. The animal's gaze
is impudent, love's metaphysics
is its own in a bereft air and compensates
for what the stars used to know. The price.
It is worth the price. It is worth it,
for it must be worth it.

✣ Then Philosophy

The inch worm is crystal clear
With this green. Touch it with doubt
And the world succumbs at once,

Vanishing into the bruise.
The municipalities
Of idea that replace

The history of inch worm
Brilliance are the expert
Province of the world as it

Quite departs. Is supplanted.
Memory muses better
Of it as we make query

Of new fruit from a new world.

✿ Side View (Alumna Report)

The organism bores through,
Has side effects, everyone

Knows all about them, loses
Patience with them in time

Patience loses too, whether
To love or psoriasis.

My own complaints are private
When no ache loosens my love

Or my astonishment, no
Pain, I mean, or keen startle

Of light such as winter brings
To despised architectures

In strange bleak towns, and I gasp
As though back home with vision

Still intact, but it isn't:
Something one can learn to see

As clearly as if the loss
Of vision were another

Young horse whose shoulders swing out
Suddenly articulate

Covered with gold, suddenly
In the afternoon knowing

Balance and fire, suddenly
Coveting grace and movement

As if they were her own and
Her own news, and light rolls on.

Road to Beauty

All things are on the road to beauty
Or else how could we see them lurking
In the darkness? Something to stumble
Over in darkness is not the real—

Not that which concurs with the eyes bright
With their desire that the world exist
Reverberating in every breeze,
Blizzards, too. Witless philosophers
Deny that the farm collie knows
The blizzard, but in their youth collie
And philosopher are both giddy
With laughter, knowing in the new fall
Of diamonds because the truth sends sparks
Flying from their paws and they worship
The way their own limbs conceive beauty
In themselves. The proper nouns betray
Philosophers long before collies
Come into them; the shepherd says "Sheep!"

A dancing verb, now full of knowledge,
Sending the dog on a long sweep past
Obfuscation and the woolies come
Home, proving that for the collie "sheep"
Is a verb—hence well along the road,
The philosopher studies signposts
All day, and brings home no sheep, studies
Into the night, too, and the puzzling
Moon remains a noun, except the mind
Take up the dance, bringing the word home

To stay. Now the philosopher's mind
Is as bright as the collie's with hope,
Flings up all its nouns in a glitter
Of prayer in which all words are commands
Philosopher and dog obey now,
Swinging out on great slopes, bringing the
Real home. Performance becomes them both
As they prophesy, everywhere, joy
As fools do. As the utter fools do.

The Old Dog Now

The old dog now floats
in the earth's crust,
turning over

as I walk by
working a dog
of different breeding.

❧ Hounds

They lean
into the wind
that is kinder
to their voices

than ours are.

❧ Upon Hearing That Helen Keller
Has a Bull Pup

Everyone wants to speak to her!
Well, who wouldn't want to speak
Into the dark that may be the heart?

I can see it now—perhaps
You could too, your mind uncluttered
By the eye's perjuries—how

Only the bulldog, intent
On your heart as on a boar,

Could have stayed the course while you
Found your way out. Perhaps

You called it love in time—that
Is one way to call

What the bulldog does love
In time—in your case

It would have taken more
Mercy than mountains have just

As it did in my case—
Exactly

This dog
Is for love alone

Who walks a
Broad dog

On capable loins with
Out comment.

🌿 Going to Ground

When the rank badger spits, "DOG!"
The terrier fawns on the earth,
Falling to the eager task

Of opening, letting loose
The nourishment of vision
As if the earth exhaled food,

As if the earth could think up
A way for us to live. The world
And the earth become as one

Beneath the dog's dancing feet,
As we peer upward, mindward,
Logic's indifferent sword

Before us, holding at bay,
Above us and below us,
What her pays turn up and what

Light from her eyes meets the light
From the mother and father
Of truth as she throws her throat

Into the thought-born glitter
Of good. That good that should be
Otherwise, should be righteous.

What Philosopher

What philosopher denies
The moods of the wind and stones?

What philosopher has learned
To fear the silent oak trees?

What philosopher can with
The fullest joy shiver when

The terrier goes for sticks?
As for the philosopher,

As for the heart of the world.
So long as ideas edge

Their way between what is good
And so extreme and happy

And what is blackest evil
And so extreme and happy

Some philosophers will learn
To deny the wind and stones

Or to accept them into
The golden truth of the world.

✢ The Wax Figure Ruined

That so priceless patience gone
Into these fragments of fret
Intact where the gay figure

Was to dance: experience
Significant the first time
The curve thrusts into the mind.

As for the collie himself
Intent on the fragile shape
Of the ewe's heart where the world

Is won, or else lost as scattered lumps
Of wax replace the keen edge
Of patience we relied on.

This is how leaves regather
In the event there is a mind
For the world, the requirement

Of light. Sculpting would be
Breathing if patience lived in
Wax, or the hand's intentions

As it does in all the dogs
Moving, ever in motion, never
Stopping, more thorough than death.

Here are heart and mind at home:
The dog is dangerously
Designed to carve out his own

Breath against the bright, roughened
Bark of bronze; the proportions
Prey on the mind like desire.

Later, the trick is to stretch
Bronze out to the crystal tense
Point before the fluid break;

Until contentment curves up
Over the heart, donating
Its light to eternity.
What we grasp of sanctity
On earth we can relinquish
Sometimes, in sharp, unholy joy.

✤ The Tree That Plucks Fruit

for Robert Tragesser

The tree that from the bare air
Plucks its fruit lives forever.

All the conceits of number
Keep the air aloft. Meanwhile

The orchard that from the air
Picks out the fruit of our lives

Becomes a name for home,
An inscribing of the earth

With what lies outside the world
And is the worth of the world

For us how breathe on the word,
Fogging it up, polishing,

Navigating truth by the stars
Flung carelessly everywhere

On the ground and in the air
And into the branches where

They are caught by the motion
Of that vegetable growth.

Dark Stars

Poetry discovers truth out there
For anyone to name. Astronomers
Discover dark stars. Truth is brought up

Sometimes into the light. The surrounding debris,

Obeying no known laws, will meet up
With Truth, the unknown instigator of
Acts both dark and light, and the secrecy

In which they meet. The debris is not all ours;
The gods are as slovenly as truth
With everything that we hold dear. They shine

During disastrous storms, the chaos

Of stuttering hearts no affair of theirs.
The poets think these inelegant hearts
Can help sometimes. Hence, long ago, they

Accepted as their client the darkest star.

✼ A Subtle Gesture

A subtle gesture, an ace
Here rather than there, the sun

With a slight tic. It's madness
Not to believe in the sun

Itself instead of gold streaks
Of luck, deceptive dapples

On the floor of the forest
Favorable to our lives.

There's the desert to come that
Favors light as winning streaks

Gone mad. But light,
(Life, death) is what we see by;

Creatures that see in the dark,
Hunt in the interstices

Between the stars for what life
Leaves out, may haunt the silence

In our melodies, but love
Unlike our melodies is

Complete, sings to the creatures
That search the dark, the better

To locate the light. The light stays
And will stay, carrying time

In its sweep. We will never
Know the creatures of the dark.

Light was the least probable
Gesture of the universe

Until we and the creatures
Of the fair and the black came

To listen to, to fear, to want
In each other the limnings.

Each as delicate as fire,
Of desire at last at rest.

❧ Decorum of Time

Time is the decorum of fate.

The valley is the decorum of the mountains,
quickness
the manner of squirrels.

Relinquishment
of the mountains and the hills
the decorum of age;

greed for them
the decorum of the youth
who stands in the garden

delivered by her blue enamel days
from the secrets of the moon,
the jabbermouth of the sun,

the sexual air emptied
by his rash collapse
in elation, for time

is the decorum that
under the eaves is whispered
by the name of fate.

❧ Delight in a Seasonal Shift

Nature, red in word, sends tooth
and stance, to spread the alarm
and the creatures heed, although

innocent of language, say
the priests who deny at once
the Word of nature, knowledge

in the chittering grey brown
breast of the squirrel who leaps
with a scream when I enter

the barn, in fall, a season
of much road kill. Other priests
deny at once heaven,

hearing nature's hot red word
as a pale word of their own;
good and evil war in this way

against the heart of truth that,
by love, sustains fact's dark lock
into time as the first form

of disorder or the last
error, the one just before
the slant light, more numerous

by name than God, can appear
as something we remember,
as a cowbird's single thought

or a dove's multiple wings.
It is as if the body
were to turn into the soul,

become indivisible,
live as a word-like spear,
never be at war with thought.

It happens. Then it leaves, like dawn
paling into some moment
we have no name or love for.
Knowledge forms an arcing quest
across the terms of word, time,
doubt. This shape is our delight

in the seasonal shift
by means of which we can know
dark by light, word by nature,

nature and light by the word.

Trained Man and Dog

He is old enough.
He has catalogued
The disappointments,
Seen the stars that fade
In grim stillborn eyes.
He is not quite sure
He himself is real.
He walks toward a field
Clean with fresh mown grass,
Keeping pace, his dog
Keeping pace. He is
Full of glory as
The heavens give way
In all directions.
His dog minds their grace.

Decorum has fought
The gods of clearing
For weeks. Now the dog,
Now the man, need room.
Therefore heaven's cloak
Falls away; and time
Thus honors the dog
And the man, they who
Stood forth forever.
Heaven provided
All of the landscapes:
Rats in the dog's jaws.
Man-scent in her flews.
Flocks held by raw bared
Force, mild in her eyes.
Suitors and braggarts
Lusting for the wind.

The trained man and dog
Have their pick of gods.

See how they come,
One stride at a time.
Dangerous to all
Weak hearts, to the law,
And many prophets,
One stride at a time
To favor the fires,
Promise what they will.

All of the action
Is still at the edge
Of the clearing, its
Ordinary work
Being to forbid
Entry to the mind.
But time carries on,
With heart-reason. Hence:
Man, dog, clearing, gods.
See how the fire folds

To form the goldsong
Of the golden world.

See how near they come.

𝒜 So There Is Justice

I

                      we who
Could have called it anything
Once called it water for what

We thought of it
                  so sweet in
The throat or Virginia when

The first flake, just as fragile
As what it can make of your
Best thought on the arcing glass

Shield. Not that it's arriving
To meet you but that you slam
Into it, your intention

Diverted from how you both
Glide so as to gild. But we
Need not struggle with conscience

Or any other angel,
Curses on his thighs or not,
For we have names for water.

II

The city of justice: perfect
Articulations, forms, spires
Soaring only in extreme

Proportions beyond what state
Or greed can say about them:
Then we and our dogs are twice

Granted our birthright, are twice
Disinherited and know,
Judging what we know, how each

Snowflake history driven
Against my windshield can say
Whole republics. The scholars

Who revere gay Socrates
Get this wrong about the dogs
And the gods Plato had meant

On the way to the horse race,
The ones I met at Del Mar,
Met and faced in the homestretch.

One scholar had this idea—
That a sheepdog works for love
Of his guardian, but dogs

Work for work and trust and once
A man died, so did his dog—
Because some scholars are not

Skillful in belief though their
Gay and distant Socrates
Knew that dogs love one knowledge

To guard the sheep, another
For herding. The scholars err
Without conscience, so mistake

Gods and dogs, both theirs and ours.
The shepherds read the snowflakes
For what they are, walk with them.

III

A friend, his marriage but not
His heart in a shambles, sends
Poems disguised as learning

Disguised as journalism
In which significance shines
As though for him at forty

Belief in what we had believed
In school had become knowledge
As it is for dogs, poets,

Statesmen concealed from the state.
For water is everywhere
Instructing the throat, the grass

In Virginia. There is this decree
Given as a serpent who wants
Just a word with us. Water

Is one way of putting it
About the whole world, a gliding
Singular element of

Fruit, knowledge, names, hazards of desire.

🌿 Young Dog, Grass, and More

Her paws on the season play
News of the present movement
Of the unfallen hymn its

Resonances there for who
Can play. For who will be called
Upon to play while hearts don't.

All the light-stunned leaves forbid
The wind's chuckle to contain
Any but the most hearty

News for the young dog whose feet
Laugh with the iridescent
Grass, her whose nose laughs to find

How the wind chuckles, gold-light
In her breath. The lineaments
Of wind and dog, breathing full,

Collide just above the grass
Green edge of the lethal core
Of your world. Her clear gallop

Divulges noon pouring through,
Her eyes to gather and sow
Knowledge, as expert as joy

Residing elsewhere for no
Reason but reason's dancing
Refusals to mark out what

Cannot be marked. Her bright feet
Alter the dew with praises
Of that impermanent sheer

Sparkle, and praise will compel
Her feet in time, praise uttered
With so clear a potency

The green-edged world will reply.
The delicate truth of this
Is responsibility.

Argos who knew his master.
Ulysses who knew his hound.
We who have left them behind.

✣ News from the Dogs

The early gods say to cast
Slender and articulate
Visions out into the woods

And hope the dogs will follow
Through the fleeciest summer,
Returning with their mouths filled

With news we can make way for.
Instead, we raise gaudy flags
Into the treetops and teach

Our good red hound no more than
We know. The death of god casts
Shadows abroad. There the dogs

Can always surprise the game
Bringing us news of ourselves
If only we realize how

Deep the woods and dark the scent
As the bright season lengthens
Into the work of the mind for

Which the dogs live. God is born
Again in the news of death
So long as we let the dogs

Work in their way as we work
Our way back. How to fail: Cast
The dog at the tree you know

From childhood. Or cast the game
Yourself and instruct the dog
On his business, or cast off

The game in the wrong season
Or cast off the game. To fail
Is not to know that the game

For the dogs is what knowledge
Is when the world and the heart
Of a dog can dance out each
Moment in the mouth or cry
In the throat. In this season
Trees are flawless canopies.

Under them, no matter what
The outcomes, the dogs' return
Is the long scheduled event

Of warmth. Creatures foraging.
This is how we know the dogs
And all the other returns.

With Argos going ahead
Filled with immortality
As we are when the dogs show

The returns, the rocky quests,
To be names for each other,
The long truth of each other,

As though, at last, they were one.

Tricks of the Light

❧ Part I

That year—
  —no one was in the office—
    —and everyone turned out

to have a sense of snow

while at the edge
of the smog in California

the very edge

of the smog a young girl
hot with light
rode a stallion, just the two of them

dancing up the sun.
They were not friendless—
everyone turned out—

but it was just the two of them.
Look for them, they are
there at the edge of that idea.

How does the sun rise?
It is a trick of the light, an effect
of nameless stunt riders

who have hormones, produce
families, children
who in a scatter of plastic horses play

up the sun. And there are
major talents, also nameless,
who dance it up, dance it down again,

so they can dance up and down
the length of time or circle it
against philosophical attack.

Their names stand
against the brutal thrusts
of the tongue, live in the light forever.

The pragmatic reasoner
could not help the light in his voice.
The social reformer

cannot prevent the light
anymore than the hoodlums
who run the country can

prevent the light from running away
to join the young girl
on her stallion.

She can't help the light either.

It is not only the philosophers who are helpless.
The light, too

that I find in your eyes, with which
the movie producers are so cunning

cannot stop itself—that is
Shakespeare's cunning against
the light, that he knew not

to stop it, and it loved him.
        Not that he said so.
                That lie of his about magic!

Think of the scientists. Think of all the real;

let the light come through the corn
as it will. Their eyes twinkle

in the penumbra of vocation. (Nurses.)
Twinkle as you will

or take it seriously; you must keep reading
the book, watching

for the stunt riders because
the light has a hunger for geometry;
has had for centuries, wants

in its light-bound heart
to reconcile infinite
straight lines with circles.
We wanted to know how
the straight line of light off the snow
became the sun, not crooked,

but so full of dimensions only a young girl
or a very old woman or a man
on a horse can dance the matter

and only a mathematician can name
what your heart rises to
as you come around again,

perfecting the arc
that understands itself
alone in the universe,

though it is not, though
it is peopled with truth

like a city and peopled
also with deer and with Dorset lambs
who, their hooves aware—

deer and sheep—of each other
prefer not to mingle
so as to keep their view

of coyotes
on the one hill, sheepdogs
on the other, clear.

To keep the view clear. An arc
is not a circle

but it strives. The arc
of the hill brings the sheepdog Jet
to the sheep in whose hearts

the circle is tight and warm.
The sheepdog's heart has already seen
the farther perspicuity.

The dog remakes the sheep as the focal
of the parabola that marks out for them
the insinuations of safety,

which insinuate also infinity;
the advanced dog sees all of this
and lifts the sheep

into the completion of light;
the sheepdog has seen all of his
and so must fetch the sheep, being

flawlessly helpless against
the higher good. This syntactic unit
of what the sheepdog has seen

commands also the shepherdess
even at dawn, real one

in blue jeans, *Science Diet* logo
on worn jacket, voice so soft you'd swear
she knew something. She won't quit,

but is there hope for the hoodlums
whose helplessness against the light
is never overcome

except by waiting? They won't wait. I won't.
You can say that your heart
did it on purpose, the seasons,

everything. This is what your heart did
as helpless as the sheepdog Lark,
so quickened with knowledge

the scholars flush to see her, even
as though they realized Shakespeare

had to start somewhere. So does the sheepdog
while the word "instinct" follows her
every move almost

defying purpose like a theory
of color. The purpose of light,
theories of light,

is to circle time. The hoodlums
cannot prevent the light
running with the young girl,

the theories, the sheepdog's heart;
the scholars blushing from their glimpse
of the sheepdog on their televisions,

it all leads somewhere
like an arc allowed
to become a circle,

as if it could be prevented.

Philosophy pitches everything she has
against the light about to unfold
in the sheepdog's heart. The shadow

is merely another felicity
of the light. This is
Kant's triumph and the ill

to which all our acts are heir.
You try it! To stop the heart
of the sheepdog you must see

the higher good as she does,

and circle it, good square flanks
will give shape to the view,
that's the only way, but the sheepdog Lark

is quicker than you are. Pity
for the singer only quickens the aria
until time is contained

in a way that satisfies
even the Dorsets as the Border Collie
makes her attributions,

stopping so fast, beyond reason, she quite
reassures the sheep, her start
and her stop relentless

against time, which quails back
in rapture. Philosophy
emerges now, knowing everything

and with a pot of gold to boot
while science, blank, forgetting to twinkle,
blinks at these tricks of the light,

blinks earnestly to engage
the rainbow that is no longer
free for everyone. It is your own

rainbow. Beneath the earth
with its busy damp changes the rainbow
completes itself as though we were root

and gold

becomes a color and a substance
on a palette. The philosopher spends
the gold on more philosophy so that

the arc makes its leap
as immortal things will; that glitter
is the purchasable glitter

of the dilations of time. The philosopher
is for the nonce as quickened with knowledge
and swift with it all

as the sheepdogs Jet and Lark—and don't forget
young Bill who is coming along
though his flanks

are still too sharp and tight. Honing
in too fast is a typical fault
of the young dog. Famous

dogs, key dogs in the family
have started this way. The young child
flings his plastic horse too

carelessly but a major talent
is there to circle time. The shepherdess
worries that Kep

is not eager enough to get
to the head of his sheep, "Whose sheep
are they, Kep?" she

chastises, and in like terms
we are all scolded
for failing to own the light. What

comes next will decide the matter; Kep
gets backup from Mack
thus goes on with his lesson

this time. He needs to learn to stop
without losing heart, a puzzler
says the shepherdess, who

sends him again: "Get back!"
hoping he will learn
to disobey her, and he does

several times bringing in the sheep
in an untidy scamper but surely
from out of sight in the woods

that mark off the other hill,
the one with coyotes, remember them
in your prayers,

every one of them a songdog. The aria
only quickens in the light
and in the darkness; speed

becomes a goddess on a spring day
when the gods are otherwise
engaged the whole length

of the pasture. The aria
only quickens in the light
in the darkness where

pity drops globules.

✂ Part II

Simultaneity
glitters in each stride
refuting nothing until

nothing is lost
as the young Airedale
crouches at once to leave

the earth and meet
the ball, varmint, mink,
dumbbell, raccoon, it's all one

gift. Our cruelty
and our kindness with the dogs
might as well be one god

aslant to the truth; one god
in many gestures, many gods
in one gesture, that's the local report,

which is not to say that we are lost
when time comes in, but there can be
one dazzling gesture, two

dazzling events joined in birth.
One gesture, many gods
and a law

of the light at its best
and for us the law is one gesture,
infinite events

for all we know, which
out here in the training field whose heat
draws the breeze in from the Sound,

electricity from the sky,

light from your eyes,
dogs across the hurdles,
thirsty, drought-friendly birds

to the galvanized water bucket,
and don't forget light from the sun
(the girl at the edge of the idea),

more than we can count. The brightness
gestures at each dog on each retrieve,
each handler sending,

opening to the dog's knowledge,
where heat compels
event known here

by eager report
in the Airedale's eyes, known
in the mortality

that settles everywhere
when a certain gesture
goes missing. Think about the scientists

trying to protect the sun
from itself and the earth
turning headlong to offer itself

in every particular
to the heedless sun while the dogs
elaborate what the light has to say.

Some of the handlers:
they become accustomed
to being as careful

as the earth and the sun
twined into a single incomprehensible
imaginary number for force

suggest they should be
with their dogs, with
the urgent report; the ways

the eager reports fail to come in
when the field fails to draw up
the murmur of contrasting coolness

from the Sound. In just one gesture
of the earth heat and coolness
come into being leaving

between them the space that is
the dog's single gesture, multiple
event. In the movies

the dog's command of what philosophy
pitches herself against is a German Shepherd
in noble profile on a roof, just about

to leave the roof, meet the bad guys
head on, a trick Rin Tin Tin
took seriously in the good old days

of insufficient safety
on the set. Rin Tin Tin
despite the belief of millions

was real. The most deft of deities
were required for the delineations
he seized as his own. In the middle

of all of this the love story
pacifies the psychologists
of the practical griefs, diagnostic critics of pap

against whom philosophy,
practical in her fire with her tribes
singing for war,

pitches her highest
with the punch of success at last
even though, and meanwhile, from the altar

of the real Rin Tin Tin with final victory
out of reach of philosophy leaps from the roof, giving
his profile to the sky, his teeth

to the grimy outlaw throat. His sense

of precisely how infinite his boundaries were
was fully achieved; he died
one day, in mid air. His eschewal

of fear gives philosophy
the wrong idea. In that eschewal
he left the earth, greeted the air, thought

bearing him aloft. Our dogs'
exercises in reality, over
hurdles and down the gauntlet

of the other dogs in a friendly class, a rehearsal
for meet and happy conversations
with their own immortality. Their eyes

glint off the commands we send them
as off a meal of fresh meat, whole grains,
grass and pasture. Philosophy

almost missed that one, the ethics
of rapture in dogs who rehearse
for the felicitous performance

that can without warning fling
dogs and handlers
into the center of art

not far from the hearth. Nobility
feels the gravity of the hearth,
learns to work with it

as with the beloved enemy and might be
a part dingo, huge and golden in a story for girls,
who kills his brother in defense

of her father's sheep. One gesture,
many events, occasions for time
to alter course. In Phoenix

Arizona an Airedale named Josh
learns to retrieve with the aid of water (the swimming pool, cool
and blue and artificial in defiance of the light

that cradles Phoenix like a rock) learns to retrieve
and to like it, to burn it down through time. All of this about dogs
takes you to the center of gravity,

just as horses might, or angels or what
glints from the scientist's eyes, but only the dogs
can locate the center

without a map. Angels
use the dogs for reference; and the young girl
finds an accommodating wood

for her noontime ride and goes out
with her hound beside her. Love's architecture
says everything

at once so that the master's heart
soars in love, with something
besides love invoking the image

of wings. God didn't create dogs, he
already had one says the legend in the training manual
attributed to some Indian

who was supposed to know. Young Comet
burns her way, needs
only reminders, while the tenderest pup, Tango,

named for radio call signs, emerges sleepily
into the light he and his master
cannot help but host in their faces

even as fall ruffles the dogs' coats,
burns up the oak tree. Dixie, Shepherd,
tawny, a trooper,

started out pretty rough. Sampson
is the Bernese who has hold of everything,
who waits until he sees the whites of your eyes

before greeting you. There was supposed to be
some Indian who was supposed to know all of this
before we did. Stella, white poodle,

shedding light as she makes *gaiety*
into a new word. Quincy, little blond,
started feral, brings in the dumbbell

on a long laughter of legs, Quincy the big
Black Labrador cross, we had a time of it with him
and the cows. We still do

have a time of it with him as he steps
over pools of light, one, two, one two,
knowledge in his stride. Supposed to be someone

who knew all of this ahead of time. Curry, Yorkie
the color of curry and with spice
in her heart, is starting hot

for the dumbbell, big heart
on tiny legs and Maxine, the Bouvier
nails those scent articles, though

she wanders in her mind sometimes
since her surgery. Some say it is a kindly
psychologist who knows all of this

ahead of time. One of these days Jack,
the Czechoslovakian Circus Dog
who was on death row, will perfect

his backflip; already he tosses light
over his shoulder as though
it weighed nothing. Chili,

the other Bernese, says something in the softest dog
tongue, and there isn't a dog for miles
who hasn't answered back with a growl, "He

never does that!" they say, and Chili
continues doing recalls down
the length of a gleam. No one

human can hear what he says, but we all laugh
even Martha who is tired of other dogs
riling Sampson's moral sense. Johanna,

full of passion,
sends, glorious, her bull pup Belle
to infrequent but epic retrieves, such

a history to it, you'd think
they were wedded, which
they are, in a single seriousness

through every insinuation of light:
we gasp to see Belle, a fawn blur,
nail the dumbbell as though it were truth. Sam,

coonhound, hasn't been broken
of baying (Pat doesn't want her
to stop) adjusts to being asked

to act like a poodle and plods
meditatively, her heart a deep baying,
announcement of more than landscape. Transfigurations

dapple the air like knowledge
in the dead of winter with snow
like a sixth sense on everything. In the snow

we find out just how good Sampson
is at that blind retrieve, pretty damn good, you tell me
who knew ahead of time. If it wasn't

God, it could have been that Indian
seeing it all from shore. In each stride
simultaneity glitters until the ground

is strewn with light. This happens regularly
like creation, brand new
by definition. The true dog trainer

gives it all away, saying, God
didn't create dogs, he already had one,
in whose single gesture every event

became many gestures of the one god
many creatures in the one gesture,
in a legend; for us the

trained dog stands at the center, the
trained tongue too and upheavals
when notice bears on the periphery.

Part III

Usually we're done
before darkness falls, not
always. But there are seasons, too,

when you can arrange
to know only one direction of the sun. A shadow
is half the darkness or else

is half full of light; we're grateful enough
for the shade of the oak tree
in those seasons when you can pretend,

if you arrange it so, that the sun
is always on its way up
or down, going toward comfort

as if "dawn" were the best word
in your own language
and always arriving,

or as if "dusk" were such a word
as comfort is compounded of, as
a student of evolution

might find it to be, seeing
always the dawn of knowledge,
the ease of sleep,

in the shards of bone. Science startles the dogs,
like our other reveries which they wait out,
impatient for us to intervene

and accept intervention
as the earth's due. Throughout the winter
we read generous volumes

on the sense of beauty and still the dogs
gleam in their skins. The scene of reading
is in this way illuminated,

located as the time and place always
of the dilatory handler. A dog's contentment
can only go on so long and then

there's the glowing girl on her horse,
and the dogs, restless with light. As we respond
the word *love* forms in our mouths. Nothing

has been found to improve
on that one, even when the light
gets up to speed and the mind

tastes just right, congratulating itself
as though it could move at the speed
love maintains in his lordly

stroll among our meadows. Love's glow
can be seen as the enemy of the light
for us, though for the dogs

love and work are at peace
like the scraps of a mind
swiftening into a whole. But this summer

of dawns has been a little odd, a patina
like a warning being the first sign
of light on the maple trees

and the sparkling young Airedale bitch
is subdued. You stub your toe
and your heart and forget the bug spray

and the flies are ferocious
no matter how sweetly the light plays
out the haunches of the dogs

as they leap loyally away
over the hurdles, mountains. Love's glow
catches on the dog's teeth firm

on the dumbbell as she returns. Science,
as moody as ever, identifies
the enemy, performs a hit and run,

taking the light with her until
the song calls it back, or a handler,
fresh from the first

invention, so fiercely fails
to be instructed that her dog
leaves the earth behind

long enough to collect the stars
in his mouth
and return with them. These same stars

ornament the long song
of love and the whimsical name
of my young Airedale bitch

whose subdued prancing
justly ornaments the light
of an overly-precise season.

Subdued now, the dogs teach us
new evasions of the dangerous moods
of reason. If feeling would do it,

or reason, there would be no need
to evade the liaison between the two,
but it is only the soft light

lifting the throat of the young Airedale
into the good
that keeps us from the morass; the sooner

we admit this the better, for until we greet the light
pain and morality have at us
working at will as though the will

were food for death—pain, pleasure
and morality fill in the marshy spaces
left behind when we leave the light.

Reason and feeling and pleasure,
will and morality
join philosophy

in her misguided and self-destructive pitch
(not the new one, the one made
centuries ago)

and love emerges from the fray
as a form of light. Unnerved
reason makes her play

for light and wins through
joining love in a reversal of fate,
snatching pity away before the aria

quickens beyond what we can tell
about the singer. There. The light
is steady for the nonce. Into the night

someone reads aloud and takes it slow.
A dog is a wolf or a young coyote.
A dog is a case of neoteny become useful.

The rest is tricks the light plays with your heart.
The heart strains against the grace of reason.
The dog evolved into our waiting hands.

Our nature is doom for the duration.
We are fated to rumors of war.
There is no excuse for the seasons.

The seasons have no excuse for dogs.
The dogs turn, the wind straightens their coats.
There is no excuse for the wind.

The dogs wait to tear our waiting hearts.
The grace of reasons empties our hounds.
Hounds are nothing, but the aria

quickens beyond the tales we can tell
about the singer. But. There. The light
is steady again and the dogs work well

into the dusk, still catching it up
and tossing it between our eyes
so that we are stunned into seeing them

and can keep the light from harm
at least until dusk becomes nightfall,
and there are tales of sheepdogs

bringing the sheep
out of the night-strewn gully,
for example, or from the night-

consuming hill. There is always more
for the sake of which the dogs are restless
even as they second our contentment,

as some of them do,
containing the light delicately,
prompting us to praise, "Good

old dog, asleep by the fire," and it's true
that a search and rescue dog
has to study to stay awake

for that task, which is beyond
the mere requirements of light,
stretches the seams of things

so that even with the dogs, morality
slips back in, sliding
by philosophy yet again

just as she lifts her throat in joy
oblivious to the sheepdog
slipping over terrain

philosophy does not care
for the lines of, a terrain
that argues a difficulty

only the sheepdog, bred
in the hills, can read as one
contour of thought. You can outlive

almost anything but this, thought's
recognitions of what outlasts
the seasons—call it light,

what thought is bound for
but can't get to alone, much less
navigate unless by the stars

caught in a dog's mouth,
which is why proof is a particular
movement in a room

unless it is a dog or a child or a lover
or an angel proving true
to time, one way

to draw out an arc
until it closes, containing time
like an unborn child.

The Border Collie does not announce
the unsoundness of the world,
but the hounds do, bawling out long

from one end to the other
of the legend. Time is contained
in this case

in the flews of hounds
for whose sake the kill
is mercy. Unsettled,

the neighbors buy a new car,
build fences and laws
about the fences until the whole land

is posted with closure dates, yours
mine and the hounds'. In philosophy
the sound is everything until

vision's gerrymandering manages
to contain the announcement
of the finite

in the infinite, the unsoundness
lurking even in the bright gestures
that leave and arrive

at once commanding
both ends of the worm of time.
Here the aria quickens

with renewed purpose
as the dogs glance and shrug
as if at a coyote bitch

in season, come to partake
of shelter, or as if at a radio
tossed from an overburdened sled—

there are sled dogs found in all phases
of the ice who can hear
"gee" and "haw" but never

a command to halt and no matter
how snow-blind the musher
she can never see well enough

to call a halt, hence brakes
on the sled and the awesome X
of the harness. Unsettled

city folks try to call a halt,
too, throwing the shadow of death
into the path of the sled

and naming it for law and ethics
as if that could make words harden
the way ice does at forty degrees

lower than the point fingers
can make out Braille. The aria quickens
with renewed purpose,

calling after the dogs. Their names
a comfort to the singer who, shorn of our pity,
pitiless as the notes reach to

the light and hover there
covering the scrabble of history
with a lifelike blanket of truth.

✺ Part IV

Proof is all in the mind,
taking all of the mind
away from the dogs;

the uncanny mocks us and the sky
blue or umber or just before a tornado
green with a fury of skin mocked.

The sky looks back
like a mirror
and the trick boomerangs

for us but not for the dogs
whose knowledge of their own feet
brooding over the terrain

is as swift as love. To quicken
philosophy with knowledge
is to leave proof behind

in a litter of desire. The dog in the mind
seeks the body and finds what was lost;
seeking is finding

pictured as some extremity
of risk and survival, some stunning
anguish of effort teetering

on the edge of an idea. This
is how we like to think sometimes
and more power to us. Compare

the bureaucrat on the telephone
with an elderly shepherdess—
shouts her into tears

because that is all he can do as
he has forbidden his dogs
to own the light. Their disobedience

passes for presence. The voice
of the bureaucrat
comes off on your hands

and sticks there, also
in the back of your mouth
as you overhear him

everywhere vandalizing the fire. He
is nature and time and desire staled
and must be overcome

and is, every time a dog
moves like silver into a work
that speaks, like the gesture of proof

or an aria, beyond the death
of the brightest young Airedale
glimmering like hope

on the horizon of an arc
that has not yet closed
off the leap. Why the bureaucrat

cannot know the dog with stars
caught up in her teeth
like a song, is a question

for the bureaucrat or else
the high giggling moon,
shamed when an idea leaps

across a shadow, making noon
cavort among the oak leaves
until proof comes round at last

to merge with the leap, no,
confess a history of leaping,
become one with the steadiness

of the sheepdog's eye as the promise
of language flickers
at the edge of vision.

The dogs have helpful impulses
but are in the end more hard
than soft, more hard

than time. They tear through
all lights, even this golden one
of early autumn,

scattering joy everywhere,
circling back neatly
to scoop it up again,

closing the equation down
on time, which retreats,
defeated again. The air lifts

at midnight
in support of the stubborn tissue
of dreams.

Curry's style is solid
as she snaps up the dumbbell
as if it were an idea,

and the bureaucrat has no say
in this or in the way Quincy
takes one stride for four

when the spirit is in him,
more and more often
in the golden weather.

Chili tumbles
to the idea of work,
caught up for the nonce

in the reality
that defies moral theory,
though he will slip again.

Quincy the Fair and Dixie
leap out, Look! only
an angel can stop them now,

but the angels know
what the bureaucrats never will
and let the dogs be

in their leaping. No one
outside of a thriller about the dead reborn
is tough enough to know the rest,

how by day and by night
the bureaucrat in the heart
twists against the stars

as if to placate
and nourish the shade
that snatches at the dogs

without hunger, with only
the corpse of lust
for inspiration.

That corpse, disguised now
as nature, tears at the woods
behind the dogs,

disguised now as time,
now as friendship gone sour.
The bureaucrat's corpse of lust

occasioned by the dogs' triumphs
over time and history,
which for the nonce will do

until one of us manages the turn
toward form that was promised
at the dawn of reason.

When it became a necessity of logic
to deny that dogs are shadows,
logic took the form of love

for those who loved her
in secret: Wordsworth
blanketing the mountain

with rose-glowing thought.
From within the glow
proof pirouettes

and with a glancing kiss
trips the bureaucrat
on his way to the phone.

Proof is all in the mind,
the mind is all in the world,
the world is a star

caught in a young bitch's teeth
just as she is learning the grab
of the heart that sends her past hurt

into her work, leaving doubt
in the dust of regret
that stains the bureaucrat's breath.

Praise sings in the work
needing no comfort until night
like a promise broken

falls away. But night, unlike
the bureaucrat, if only for moments,
yields to the light that scatters

everywhere in, say, California
when the young girl or an old man
on the stallion or a mare or a gelding

paces out the entire length
of the edge of the very idea
of sunlight. This week

is as blind as any corpse,
tottering through horror,
the unburied thought

of time, or money, or
brute voice to shout
the elderly shepherdess into tears.

The virtue of a thing
is its function. Consider
the bureaucrat, dear Plato,

twisting against the stars.
Plato considered, so Socrates
brings violence into the cave

with the reports of truth. But
somewhere in the desert, secret
reaches of the mind,

the bureaucrat
gets boxed into a canyon
alone with a dog and

utters a single, solitary
word of praise,
his dog a blessed cat in Kipling;

then there are two words, more—this
is one way out,
back to pastures and fresh hay cakes.

The virtue of a thing
is its function. Consider
the bureaucrat, dear Plato,

dancing against reason
navigating at last by the stars
caught in the dog's mouth, hungry now.

Navigation is an art, so
consider reason
studying how to woo joy in folly,

which is a fixed mark
and so the enemy of time,
the mightiest huntress of time.

Get the timing right, the praise
of your dog, receive the crisp stars,
do that

day and night and thus
give time a miss, here
god is at last empowered—

the god who already had a dog—
and the world and the high heavens unfurl
spilling out the word "gift"

for the philosopher
who picks up on it, drops it,
picks it up again,

learning a rare light step or two
in time to dance out
the whole length of the contradiction

gaiety whispers busily,
skimming it on the bold breeze
that riffles across the dogs' throats.

Speculations on the weather
futures out the present
so that language can promise

that there had to be someone
who knew it from the start,
as if your heart did it, the stars,

the unfurling, the dog's feet,
the wide cloud of light
in which we pitch our camp.

✃ Part V

Praise and serendipity
set the stars atop their globes,
the breeze across the field,

the birds to flight and rest,
the dogs to work
at the edge of intellect,

where "Twirl right!" and "Over!"
subsume the mysteries of time.
Serendipity

wears a magic cloak and can play
in public, with no one the wiser,
so relentless is meaning, but praise

in a world skewed—
praise in a world of hurt, praise
in a world of perversion and the cruel

delusions of time and the glare
of morality
must work in secret

or disguise itself as say
a faithful robot,
a code of conduct,

a technique, an illness,
a plea for help
or a scientific theory of light

constructed in the form of a massive sphere
from which time cannot escape.
Praise is the trick effect

that gives meaning, that glow
we learn to see by. Praise
in wartime redeems

us by being a voice
singing in the wilderness and if
it betrays us thereby we learn

a peculiar chariness
with our beauty, like a cardinal
in winter trading love

for a fierce slash of color
against the white of death.
Praise betrays everything

if untutored.
But stand amid the shreds
of redemption, shards

of stale promise
as among the clouds and listen
with the acutest new ear

for a word of praise
that will repeat, good,
good dog, good the murmur

good the resonance therefore well done,
the dog's leap beyond herself
and a twirl and flash

of a toothed belief. Now
that praise is lighter than air,
breathe its safety

even from the truths
you stand among, the debris
of fate. The young Airedale

twirls again hard
in defiance of the deft ground,
taking the clouds with her,

riding reality
like a word of praise
made flesh.

The sheepdog, see
on a long cross drive
heeding the bright whistle

that slips by the birds
as if that drive toward truth
could sing him home.

The greatest dogs
are careless of praise
casting its words

before us; they can be mistaken
for psalms. For great mistakes
of heart-scattered psalms

are another occasion
for the leap that sheds time
like rain on a doughty field.

Meanwhile the shepherdess
all the while curving her voice
into the murmur, good, good

and steady, steady, despises
the dog who returns
to the handler in praise

and for praise, her sternness
and sweet whistles coming
from another country

in the clouds. Be instructed here.
In 1939
when *Heil Hitler*

was a call to the good,
Auden wrote about praise
from learned prisoners.

Now whisper under the gun:
a dog is praised so softly
in Phoenix cradled

in that rock-hard light
that no one hears, even when
there is no one there to hear.

Whom can we praise?
Not the blue heron aloof
in the suddenness of that beauty.

We can praise the dog and the horse and the cat and the lover and
    the wind
and god, and no one must overhear
or the world will end

as it does hourly
in that confusion of mind confessed
in the High Holy

terror that prompts authority
like a boil on the voice
of the social reformer

outraged at the exuberance
of the sun,
constant stranger

to the heart. The heart!
a poetic conceit
that misses praise like an enemy

with poor aim, but for the dogs
the light of what they strew—
the heart for them a grammar

beyond time. Praise,
never more than a small voice (accompanied),
transumes thought

in its knowledge
sprung from vision
alone, no symbol

intervening between the small voice
and the exuberant dog
and the leap.

Only here does trope
let us be, for the moment,
in the eternity

the philosopher nods
hopelessly away from,
realizing always the remote

reach of the heron's flight
from the one sanity
where the dog frisks

complete in candor
as though our words
were the smile of the world.

Or the dogs works,
complete in candor,
with an achieved eye

for the sheep,
point of balance;
balance and power and style

and a fastidious lift
that brings the sheep
afloat on beauty

down the subtle field.
The sheepdog's prompt eye
is not candid

until years of work
and the shepherd's whistle
sweetened by knowledge

become at last the word
for praise, the nod
of chance when

it becomes real, consorting
with the uncanny
of the dog's achievement

(the vessel of meaning).
On that sweet whistle
the sheepdog's virtue

sweeps the hill,
gilding the aching stretch of time,
enclosing it all.

No restless crowds
become weightless with comfort
in the sweep of virtue

which barely brushes
the surface of time,
but it brushes, barely,

the whole surface
for the nonce and even
a philosopher, alone

on the hill
can see that beauty, afloat
before the dog's eye.

Here the violent smoke of sin,
fatigue, evasion and the certainty
of the loss of love

become one
with the clarity of the air
that parts for the dog

like water. Time rallies
from the blow of praise;
love dies into the air

like a season, thoughts
of supper blend
into submission

to sleep, where dreams
ravish the dark. But the word
for praise is a guide

in that angled anguish
of light, making its architecture
rise, a thing

our valor can own to.
And so we rise,
each of us to brush

our region of time, our dogs
shedding glitter that gives
an outline to time.

Sometimes someone claims
the light in their teeth,
catching up what the dogs toss

and sometimes someone sees
it happen, overhears
that swift bright grammar

which is a spark
prancing at the speed
of love. The world

accepts her new center,
the light consorts
with the heart. Knowledge

arcs with a word
for praise to join
love, hammer out pity like silver, and it is good,

the glitter, good
the tricks that restore,
for a while, the immortality

of the sun, good the truths
you stand among, good
the word of praise made

to flash as the dog
twirls again, hard and gay
in the ablest of airs.

from *Nervous Horses* (1980)

✤ Prayer

    imagine me, imagine
the red
       horse, that we
   in our riding
      Dance
  to your Name, as

Flame selects us
  joyous
         to the stamp
  of you, flesh
  of you, breath

✤ Glitter: A Critical Essay

The evil men do gets after them
In their dreams, or on certain mornings
When the relentless O Clock! of the

Clock is no friend. I mean nothing by
This, just insomnia, drunkenness,
Oversleeping, feeling a slight shock

When the Famous Critic maligns our
Friends. Feeling that shock must be paid for
In the usual way and perhaps

As dramatically as ever:
Here soul wrings her hands not to
Wash them, but to cry like hypocrite

Readers, "Not again!" To notice how
Old this sin is, is to fall asleep
More easily and to love our friends

As friends, not fathers. But to see how
Radiant Love is, is to come awake
More thoroughly, and to love our friends,

At last, as lovers. The sign of love
Is not the cross, filthy with tears and
Blood, but the cross burnished, gilded, rare.

That we may sometimes want to see a
Cross dazzle, and not think of sin, is
No minor blessing, granted by no

Foolish poet, but by the first Word
Of Man, that comes to us rightly
Radiant, ever gently, and pure.

Riding a Nervous Horse

A dozen false starts:
You're such a fool, I said,
Spooking at shadows when
All day you were calm,
Placidly nosing the bushes
That now you pretend are strange,
Are struck with menace.

But he shuddered, stubborn
In his horsy posture,
Saying that I brought
Devils with me that he
Could hear gathering in all
The places behind him as I

Diverted his coherence
With my chatter and tack.

Indeed I have stolen
Something, a careful attention
I claim for my own yearning
Purpose, while he
Is left alone to guard
Us both from horse eaters
That merely grin at me
But lust for him, for
The beauty of the haunch
My brush has polished, revealing
Treasures of edible light
In the shift of hide and hooves.

Ibn, Who Wouldn't Be Caught

He had read of rhythm in the Book
Of the Free-Thundering Hooves. He dodged
My hands, my ropes, my notions
Exactly as though no human
Ever fed him.

Eating wild, running wild,
Horses moving like pillars
Of light parting the silver glint
Of Sinai sands—he claimed
Those rhythms, did small grey Ibn.

I laughed. Ibn who?
Son of what Wild Grey
Eminence? Ibn!

Ibn Abu I am, the son
Of my father, Ibn I am!

He tossed his mane
In the approved way,
Banging his head on the posts
Of his corral, banging
His frail tame hooves
On the artificial ground we
Both got tired of. Pillars
Of light? I teased. With mares
Like flowers at your feet?
And you a flower at the feet
Of the virgin spring?

Yes! He whickered, glowing
With the lovely rage of it all.
That spring! The spring of my kind
In the holy grasses. He
Had a long poem to say,
A poem of a horse
No one could catch, but he

Suffered, as I do, from
The wrong audience. I
Caught him and we will learn
A new song by and by.

Rebreaking Outlaw Horses in the Desert

"We study the behavior of animals because . . . our observations are not
complicated by the social relations between subject and observer."
—B. F. Skinner, "Why Organisms Behave"

Crowded out of barns
That glowed with money, we
Met in the August night,
Hiding from the death
That broke the desert air
At dawn with the first sun.

The horses came haggard,
Rough and dangerous,
Maddened by the fumes
From sour pools of wines
And loves spilled in
Mythological mornings,
Stirrup cups, garlands
Of roses for the sweating
Necks of winners, jockeys
Broken under horses
Who fell from the weight
Of clumsy legends, trainers
Dying with an urgent
Plea to the pale round
Priest who hears, "Depend
Upon it that Eleanor's
The hell of a mare!" We thought
Our own myths were safer;
What we meant, dreaming
In caves bleached by noon,
Was horses, dancing, all
Our senses sweetly ordered
In the lift and fall of hooves.
Prophetic rhythms drew us
Beyond detail, we thought,
Riding the horses. Cruel
And murderous by day,
Their hooves at night sang
And held us. Full
Of their knowledge, we left
Ours, led out of time,
The mortal rhythms of breath.

They all bowed and danced
To the laws of love
And cadence, all but the black
Mare, the crazy black
Mare who hated us
Beyond our powers, into
Herself, and what she flung
To the ground was herself.

Refusing the truth or any
Healing light she lay there.
What came from her ears then
Was blood, from her nose,
Blood, from her eyes,
Light. Some old bond
Between her kind and mine
Seemed broken then. Not lost
In the artistic mists of shows
And racing meets, nor in
The guilty breaths of Daddy,
Priggish, signing things
While old Merrylegs
Is loaded into a dank
Wagon (the children are
At school in these scenes),

But dashed contemptuously
To the ground, claimed by the mare
And tossed aside, her last
And only clarity.

✒ Daedalus Broods on the Equestrian Olympic Trials

It should have been a preparation, this
Crouching to watch the Prix des Nations,
Greedy to know every stride, the soft
Sink of hooves feeling the fluid ground
In rhythms so well known we count them in
Our sleep. Thus: one . . . two . . . three . . . Go!
At *Go,* throw your heart over the fence.

These riders know the moment of flight; a horse
In flight seems to know the passionate
Collection and release of time, the dance

That first set the universe to spin
And caused the stars to gather prophetic shapes
And hold them in their steady turn. We have
Technique and flight as givens, but we can see

The exact scope of the leap and the spread
Of wings only on certain frosty nights
When in the pasture or among the stars
One shape emerges among others as
The suggestion of if not the actual
Wingéd Horse. So we retire to caves

And potter in the dark with formulae,
Experiments, and tools abstracted from
The airy patterns made by birds, their
Flutterings a teasing help because
They are familiar. We work, brooding on
What we saw or thought we saw when one
Splendid horse of all the best of splendid
Horses claimed, with distracting passion and skill,
The prize of nations, the Cup. Technique and flight

Are givens. *At this level of competition,*
Drones the announcer, *to have participated*
Is enough. But is enough an honor?
It is the leap timed for the light, flashing
In the Steward's hand, that raises meaning,
Stamps it on graven records, claims the Cup

And the honors. The rest is talk, random
Fantasies of idle grooms who rant
And covet and babble in their cups. We think
Technique and flight are ours until our own
Sacred animals fail, irritably paw
The rockslide. Is this flight? It is high
Enough and time for it. We leave
Our subterranean broodings and emerge
On the sunny hillside, having chosen

Wings of our own crafting, and take the air,
My son and I, neither gods nor horsemen

Whose hands are blessed by the weight of golden bridles,
But men whose arms are stretched and held aloft
By creaking, homemade structures much like wings.

That is the sea, below us, answering
The sun with waves that break and glitter; that
Is the morning sun, blazing, and this is flight.

Riding a Jumper

The fence, stretched out in perfect silence there,
The trees beyond and their fruit, the last of that
Long bleak season's yield, nearly shattered
In the cold of dawn. The morning stars
Had just winked out. We knew the sun by this
And by its pallid gleams outlined in frost.
The horse and I were there again, to pause
And shiver clumsily: Was this a place
To reach after awkward travels? For us
A fence shouldn't mark so fine a line
Along the legal ground, one recorded length
Of someone else's orchard. This fence should mark
A fast hard leap that we could choose to make
Or not, onto the brittle, drought-dry ground.
Already damaged and brooding, the horse and I
Scanned the fence, entranced by measurement.

Behind us in the field where the sun
Widened and spread itself as a prophecy
Of green renewing, a herd of pastured mares
Moved. We turned and saw them, large, dim,
Lovely and slow, as remote as clouds like those
That formed this bright immobile dew and stayed.
We watched their steady feet and mouths that searched
The frost for grass, tore its fabric, and all
Our passionate skills have told me less than their feet have,
Bruising the fertile ground. One time I rode here,

Under a risen sun that lifted dust
Around their hooves, passed them, jumped the fence,
And left them startled. Other times I stayed,
Voiced some loss, loosed it in whirls of dust
Or bright clarities of frost and saw
It settled in the same old miracles
Of undiminished light before my eyes.
Almost any line enclosing one
Universe or separating two
Or more will do for visions. This one serves
To bring the horse and me limping back
To measure it again, to judge a leap,
To leap, or wait, or turn to find the mares
Knee-deep in grass, irrevocably calm.

✀ The Archer

The sudden thuck of landing
The arrow made in the mark
Of the center lifted and

Loosened his skin. And so he
Stood, hearing it like many
Thrusting breaths driven to ground.

He abandoned the long light
Flight of arrows and the slow
Parabolas bows dream of

For the swifter song beyond
Flesh. Song of moments. The earth
Turned its molten balance.

He stood hearing it again:
The precise shudder the arrow
Sought and returned to, flaming.

✣ The Horse That, Trotting

The horse that, trotting with open heart
Against the wind, achieves bend and flow
Will live forever. So far, so good,

But they never do, until too late,
Bend properly and time spreads from
The momentary hesitations

Of their spines, circles their tossing necks,
Falls from their teeth like rejected oats,
Litters the ground like penitence.

This is where we come in, where the drop
Of time congeals the air and someone
Speaks to the discouraged grass, sings to

Celebrate the formerly splendid
Horses, will call them, with some success,
Divine as their throats pulse in the dark.

✣ A Problem of Form

When a dog lies very quietly
It means that things are happening fast.

After the dog dies one feels a hard
Clarity that might be like a joy

But is brutal at the edge, like rage.
Familiarity with the facts

Tell us only that the movement and
Form of a dog are sacred, as are

These California palm trees that rise
With great certainty in parallel

Lines that mark the pull of gravity:
Announcing, claiming, yielding to the law.

✂ A Country Scene

The actual horse dragged one
Wing, and limped in pastures so
Pale with drought scrub a horse must
Grow thinner, limping there, his
Hide tamed to the duller hues
Of the pasture. Surrounding
Dull hide and dust and shabby
Scrub, the fence was merely a
Thing no horse should jump whether
Lame or no. The birds twittered
In triumph, perched on the rail
At the very top. Theirs was an
Unreasonable poise on
Rails, singing of no mistake,
Of no horses lamed by the
Foolish perfections of flight
But of the homely easing
Into air of insolent
Creatures winged only for
Their own sakes and not for the
Lethal ecstasies of song.

🌿 Against the Grain

They were never still, as rocks
Are still. The articulate
Bony core moved dreamily

In passive fluids and was
Nourished by the thoughtless shifting
Drift, that answered to the horse

To her bright delicate breath,
Her mouth's friendly ravishing.
We had ideas, watching

That drift and we pulled the wind
And ourselves taut against the
Grain of bone. This for further

Articulations. Oh, for
Further articulations.
Bone of rider, bone of horse,

Wind and horse and idea
Wrenched and flaming. Syllables
Like fire. We complain, dazzled.

🌿 Emergence

Excellently scented, the horses,
Excellently proportioned. This is
Just how they are made and no other
Fashion would suit a horse quite so well.

Their smooth forms push back tangling grass,
Reveal leafy new precisions for

Our limited sight. The undefined
Birds had chirped uneasily, but now

Exact notes herald around the forms
Of horses. What we like about them
Is that this is how they come, in peace.
What ennobles us is this watching

Of their precisions. Their affection
For the epiphanal landscape.

The Fifth Horseman

for José Antonio Villarreal

The horse is not enough; soon

A man rides beautifully,
Losing the bruises, wounds
In which speech and the need for

Speech were mercifully lost.
Pancho Villa rides in his
Mexican eternity

While women are or are not
In one's bed, and are or else
Are not a bother. Blessings

Hound the warrior; the horrors
Of battle won't keep them out
Of the moments that slip in

To a man while he's waiting
For fresh horses. And no one
Not even the Mexican

Is poet enough to stop
The relentless blessings of
Peace, the justice in desire,

The taming of fine horses.

✻ Bathing

for John Hollander

The allegory broke there
To flow past frail Midas while

Words protested their old sounds,
Their place in his throat. What song

Could have been sung? The careless
Brook retired to a bedtime

Babbling, and the king would no
Longer lend an ear, not to

That ground. Denied nourishment
He spat out the soil, his mouth

The sieve through which sifting sands
Passed, leaving unsingable

Residues of gold. What song
Could have been sung when singing

Froze the liquid word? (He would
Revive in his kingdom some

Shabby old arts of comfort,
Call for flagons, stay himself

With girls and apples.) He would
Deny Apollo and then

Elevate lowly Pan, would
Mourn Orpheus, but only

The dear flesh of him, that voice
Pleading, breaking beyond song.

✻ Waking

"It was not the vision I had."
—Gulley Jimson

Entranced, he learned what he had
To know. Now Midas, nervous
In the calm daylight, can't say
Why the divine engineer
Must, for the sake of the bleak
Requirements of the matter,
Fail, always, to sound warnings
Of the hardness of gold. The
Rosy transitory flush
Of Midas, bright with joy as
He reaches to pluck the first
Fruit of the new age, is worth
All that comes after. Visions

Of golden horses who dance,
Breaking clear waters and light
From dead stones, help us to know
In time, the cures for ailments
Caused by the concussions hooves
Suffer, meeting a truer
Hardness on the too earthly
Mountain. Collisions with
The ground tell us where to find

The ground, but the upper airs,
Even filled with distracting
Sparklings, have shown us something
Of our postures on the ground
And the shameful reasons we
Take our stands the way we do.

It is not that, entranced, we
Can leap, never having to
Pick our way up a rocky
Slope that leads only to airs
Much too hard and bright, but that
Entranced, we can discover,
Merely imagining, what
It means that those same horses,
Lamed by our hide-bound questing
And pastured now, will call out
Clearly enough. Thus guided,

We needn't fear the stony heights
Where, dazzled, we learned the fast
Revenge biology takes
On the dreamy husbandman.
Reminders of our early
Bad management crowd the low-
Lying fields and start to climb
After us, their voices harsh.

Knowing them for what they are
Is the gift Midas, silent
Against our reasoning, brings.
Now: All that glitters is gold.

✢ The Pillar of Gold

It might have been light, merely,
Pouring through windows, of a
Church, say, but for its hardness
And the way it drove on, not
Pausing, through the space I thought
I occupied. What it was:

Not gold, not light. An idea,
Perhaps, the one we have to
Entertain, in order that
We know gold and light and flesh
For themselves and for certain
Family resemblances.

✢ The Exact Role of Value Judgments in War

for Yuri Zhivago

Some things made sense, like pauses
In our best arguments. Light
Shone on our faces, just and

Soft. Roots scattered the soil, grass
Blades scattered the roots, crisp leaves
Scattered the lawns and we walked

In the evenings, admiring
That dance. The virtuoso
Moon was dressed to glow, and shone

On it all as if the truth
Never failed us. As if the
Moon would allow itself light

Forever, ready at the
Very moment any one
Of us should choose to turn a

Tranquil face upward and look
At eucalyptus trees that
Do not clutch but are drawn down

Like a lawn sloping straight up.

❦ The Singing Lesson

"Can't they see it's a horse?"
—Gautier

He listened to Orpheus
And saw, leaping against a
Background, as if tensed within
Stone or nugget, perfect shapes.
Form perfected? Well, no, form
Found to be perfect. It was his
Vision of the malleable
Heart of gold, looking much like
Love. The shapes summoned by
Song were to him like horses
In a story for children,
Worth, for their nobility,
Sacrifice, and for their truth,
Any hallucination.

Orpheus taught, and Midas
Sang, briefly, until his voice
Stopped hard against the flawless
Greed that shone in the core of
Each bright, epiphanal note.

❧ A Photograph

*(Louis Fleckenstein, "Thoroughbred-Arabians, owned by Camarilla,"
1933)*

Six captive horses, their white
Forms overlapping. In the

Interstices, a series
Of spaces where love, blackened

By chemistry to pure
Shade will answer white with black,

Black with white. You will betray
This photograph day and night

But still the horses from your
Wall will emerge, captive, bright.

❧ Science and Human Behavior

Salmon swim the hard way to their deaths,
Upstream, like stars inventing fabulous
Physics in order to explode or hint
They might. The eye at the small end
Of the telescope can't move through
Its cool equations to the other lens
And through that clarity to some
Symmetry of beyond and a seeing
Of a new kind. The skin of this

Close-mouthed creature feels strange
To the touch, but gets its only warmth
From us. Its silent gears are metaphors
For our minds, or philosophies

That promise a final focus on the true
Line at last. The stars themselves are set

To rush in a chatter and glitter down the black
Tube, to fill, beget, and transform us
For our knowing. The queer, cramped pose
Assumed for this peering reading is
Not visible to us, our vision poised
Flatly against a glass, caressing gnosis,
Like catfish in a tank that form a kiss
For the substance that keeps out the air
That may have shocked another fish to breathe.

✣ Camouflage

The Diamond Turbot so
Matches the sand around
The Pier Piling in
The Scripps Institute tank

That it is not until
He wriggles in his
Way of hiding that
We notice him at all.

The glass shows that
He and the sand are
Beaded carefully, white,
Yellow, and seemly beige.

He seems so perfectly
A part of the whole
Laying out of institutional sand that
We wonder at his shyness.

Now he shivers backward,
Digs, and is gone
From our wonder
But not from Scripps

Which we leave
Not convinced that
Under the complex surf outside
Dwell adaptive turbots

Poised in a true
Wariness, as though they too could be
Surprised by sin
With her black and violent attendants.

Next Summer

The body sufficient
Unto itself, the body

Beautiful, and tall tales,
Hounds that race the Union Pacific,

Hearts like mountains. Hearts, but
Never to be more

Than the beloved's body
Is part of it, and the wanton hound

Should be content
With his own fleas, never mind

Ticks as big as grapefruit and what the horses
Could do. Your body sufficient

Unto me: THE HORSES?
Oh, we tagged after the horses

That was all we should have
said

✿ Agnus Dei

A poem to engage the world
Smiling. The kind of engagement
Lovers have in mind. A poem
To conserve a milder meadow
And newer seasons. A poem

That gives instructions for weaving
Fragrant hammocks to catch the
Aged, the sick, the hopelessly
Competent in their daily fall
From graciousness. Oh, and we will

Want navigation manuals
For pilots flying low over
Shadow-infested valleys.
The charity of language is
Our seigneur as if God, fishing

On a fine day of purple and
Gold, sang our poor music calling
Dolphins. That would be a silver
Singing: Poems made as if God

In His mercy beckoned for them.

✖ The Fastidiousness of the Musician

My friend complained about words.
Said, how unreliable
Because not truly themselves

And so on. "A note is true
Whether alone or singing
With others of its kind—you

Never know, on the other
Hand, what a word will say; just
Look at this celebrated

Business of puns, enjambment,
The other cheap effects, fit
Only for stand-up comics."

I said I knew what he meant.
I did, too and while he talked
My hands wandered idly

Over my guitar, playing blues,
Finding those fastidious
Notes. Lingering on F sharp

On the way up, then gaily
Plucking G flat on the way
Down. It was soothing to play

While we talked seriously
And watched the white light change from
Blue to grey on the pale walls.

✢ I Was Reading Ouspensky

I was reading Ouspensky,
Once, and said . . .

Well, it was actually
My brother, Jim, who read

Ouspensky—it wasn't
Ouspensky, it was

Some such
Lunatic Slav—

And said to his friend Geoffrey,
"Geoff! It says here

That in all times and
Tongues they've named

A certain constellation,
Scorpio. Or the local

Equivalent." So Geoff
Led Jim outside,

Pointed out the glittering insect
Sprawled oracular on the wordless sky.

❧ That Hot Texas Sun

I

It is always hot
In Texas, under
That hot Texas sun.

Under that hot Texas sun?
What is this "Texas?" someone
Asked while the stylish woman
Watched her husband, a Yankee
President from Boston, slump
In the Dallas heat, his eyes
Yielding their frail Irish light
To the brutal dust that is
Pure Texas. I thought, watching
It all from California,
Of the incredible sun
In Texas, and with this thought
Came another, of rock bands,
Of how they will fail should the
Entrancing racket let up.

II

There is nothing for children
In Texas but light and dust;
Droughts marked off by floods, and wind—
Wind and slime, and tales of buried
Treasure for the finding: black
Gold. And for me the hot sun
And the faith my mother had
To live by. Pregnant with me
In forty-six, in Austin
(A university town),
In the Episcopal calm
Of St. David's there she prayed
Daily, shocking the vicar
With her wish that I be born

Beautiful. Not smart, not kind,
Not happy, healthy, or wise,
Fulfilled, or lucky. She asked,
Daily, only that I glow.

III

She owed an enormous debt
For years to Sears, Roebuck, and
Co., a debt she built
Carelessly under the hot
Sun that blasted and shriveled
All the wisdom of Texas.
She prayed in that fashion,
Combatting light with prayers for
Light, owing Sears and Roebuck
For crystal chandeliers, for
An air conditioner, for
Cunning lamps so elegant
She had to buy other, more
Common lights to see them by.

IV

She was a crack shot with a
Twenty-two, of course—Texas
Rattlesnakes are big—and I
Lived, protected by her clear
Faith, by the unruly lights
She gathered, by her good sense,
Her marksmanship, and the debt
She owed to Sears for armour
Against that hot Texas sun.

A Technical Question for My Daughter

for Colleen Lerman

I don't know where you get it, this
Growing you do; did you go out
Of the house alone, down to the
Pasture, to learn the way the pouts

And dancing of the young fillies
Set them on their legs? It is clear
You mean something by it, as when
Earlier I thrust my hands near

And then into your folds of flesh
And, infant weak and pure, you thrust
Them away, never even once
Granting that you were what I must

Clean and tend. Where did you get this
Lusting for all this competence,
Skills you had a plan for from the
Start? I should have deduced the fence

From the growing pile of rails but
They made a plausible enough
Pile of rails and I thought about
The sure way they towered, a tough

Problem in itself. You added
Speech, and began to know how sleep
May be lost and wooed; then one day
There you were, setting rails in deep

Postholes you had dug by yourself.
The laws of form draw us taller,
Slowly, and set us in our own
Universe—we say—not smaller

By an inch than we grow to be.

❧ My Father Rode Great, Silver Birds

I

He rode B-52s. He went off
Into the blue yonder on

Silver birds that leaped
Plashless into the air, then

Carried him safely home.
Those scenes

On runways: Men
In drab flight suits

Embraced by women
Whose clothes and tears glittered.

Racing to greet him,
I would mimic his limp,

Relic
Of a weather-reconnaissance mission

In 1943.
1943?

It had rained,
And he slipped, boarding

The plane, broke his leg.
It was an honorable war

Wound. Later, he built me
An aviary, nesting cages;

We came to have 150
Parakeets who not only flew,

Flashing multicolored, but also
Sang, and one of them even talked.

He is a strange man.
Perverse. Everyone says so.

II

He has a fine nose.
Once he smelled a gas leak,

Refused to fly, was court-martialed.
His crew said, "If Willie

Smells gas, there's gas."
Refused to fly. Were court-martialed.

Civil Disobedience? The next crew
On the roster took that plane.

Everyone exploded. All of them.
One mile after take-off.

A difficult man,
But with a fine nose.

III

He was a choirmaster at St. Clement's.
Transferred to another base, he built

A splendid organ in the garage,
Loaded it into his van,

Drove 500 miles,
Gave it to St. Clement's.

He subscribed to *Diapason*,
Printing Impressions, *The Bulletin*

Of the American Budgerigar Society,
Bulletin of the American

Orchid Society, and
Told me the truth when,

Right there on the runway I asked him,
"Why do the silver birds

Have such big bellies?"
I haven't seen him in years, but

Look! The great birds are leaping,
And so softly, into the heavens!

St. George and the Dragon: Piecing It All Together

for Jo Miles

One could—maybe anyone
Could do it alone, do all
511
Interlocking pieces, but
Who has the time? So we work
Together, and O the strain
On our manners! "I was just
About to do that!" "You keep
Mixing up the pieces!" "Are
You sure you don't have any
Blue dog shapes with scarlet red
Sticking out like a duck bill?"

If I have your piece, it looks
To me like the pattern of
Tiny iridescent scales
Beneath the dragon's eye. (It

Seems much easier now that Jim
Has placed the eye.) But Harry
Is the one who finds it for
You, rescuing it from my
Bemused gaze just in time. He
Saw right away the—to you—
All-important glint of bronze.
To me, bronze was a flaw in
The reproduction; to you,
The Final Piece that showed the
Saint's foot resting firmly in
His stirrup. We start to cheer—
We're halfway done! But Colleen
Points out that we've all eschewed
The difficult gleaming white
Haunch and the larger reaches
Of velvet black above the
Whole figure. Poor Marsh despairs,
But John suggests that black is
Easier, really—the eyes
Search undistracted by what
Looks exactly like the pert
Tip of the horse's left ear,
Then turns out, always, to be
Nothing like an ear, and not
Alert with a forward tilt,
But merely the flat join of
Heavy plates that guard the heart
Of the horseman. Bill says pure
Form is eye's delight, plus
Truth, but Donald won't have that,
Says if it's got no picture
On it, why bother? I think

That black is part of the whole,
But my contemplations are
Gloomy; my eye for form was
Never much good, one duck bill
Looking much like another
Duck bill to me. It hardly
Matters, black is all that now

Remains in any of our
Piles. It's come time to stop our
Chatter and consolidate:
The individual parts are
Finished, or else abandoned.

My task was to find the sharp
Silver lines of the horse's
Head, noble, yet bent to the
Saint's hand, but I've discovered
The piece with the Jewel of
The Brow to be forever
Lost. *I* didn't lose it, but
The group has charged me to find
It anyway. Ed insists
That with that piece the horse's
Version of the matter, his
Fearful and trustful glance toward
St. George, stands revealed, and that,
For now at least, the horse's
Truth is ours, that without the
Horse's vision the Saint's is
Lost to us; the piece at all
Costs must be found. Maybe it
Strayed in the months the puzzle
Lay in my closet, behind
The Ouija board that never
Worked because the pointer kept
Sticking? (The one John said to
Throw out.) Harry's task was the
Face—George's face—no pieces
Escaped him but he gobbled
Brownies as he worked, and smudged
The mouth. Bill performed his part
Flawlessly—the pointed tail
Of the beast, about to whip
Against the horse's legs in
Protest because, dying, a
Dragon does protest. But I
Suspect Bill knocked the Jewel

To the floor, and stepped on it,
Maybe carried it outside
To be lost in the garden—
Not meaning to, of course, I
Don't reproach him, but there—it's
Gone. Eleanor spent so much
Time helping the rest of us
To find our mislaid pieces
That she never completed
Any one segment. I think
She began on the dragon's
Front paws, curled so, just like a
Puppy's to its panting chest.

Still, her part got done somehow,
We may say by any or
All of us. Even the great
Haunches have been completed,
Solid and bunched to carry
The brave saint, and we've come to
Face, newly together, the
Doubtful black sky, each of us
Hoping for some communal
Vision of the same blankness,
Bent over the clueless forms.

❧ The Metaphysical Horse

I have become cautious, but

Still I should speak of horses,
Emerging and shaped just so
In the inchoate tangle

Of our truths, how clarity
Sparks in the shift of their hooves.
We saw their movement, later

Came to know that they would move
Only in the nameless air,
Only in the beckoning

Mirror where horses become
Two-dimensional figures turned
Inside out. Our old feel for

Symmetry is lost in this
Apparent reversal of
Right and left that is no true

Renvers; Glow and Valor
Arc gracefully left as they
Bend to the right rein, passing

With flawless balance beyond
The dimensions we can name,
(Carrying us) into the

Mirror we took for a source
Of light, hung in the last age
By an *Oberreiter* who

Hoped with his poor device to
Capture the numinous air
Of the riding hall, thereby

Holding the horses steady
In his hands. A priori
Horses are not real horses

But they glide as steadily
As ice in the master's dream,
In his mirror, in the hall

Where now we keep actual
Horses, consider their legs,
Their hooves, the tangle of true

Ailments—bog spavin, stringhalt,
Poll evil, founder, strangles,
Lampers, mud fever, blood worms,

Seedy toe, ring bone, thrush, cold
Back, sway-back, cold mouth, wobbles,
Wind sucking, weaving, and wind-

Puffs, and in the tangle find
Light that signifies horses,
Calm syllables rooted in

The Perfection of Nature.
Flushed with study as from sleep,
We lift our confident cheeks

To their breath and find it clear
With fragrance. Now: From the beams
The philosopher points out

That we prefer, as it were,
Seeing, that we live in a
Preference for vision our

Horses can never enter.
So we enter them, not their
Obdurate matter-of-fact

Hooves, but their movements in the
Mirror, the virtual depths
Caught in that sparkless surface

Where we are affirmed at last
In many disembodied
Bright images repeating.

Circling elegantly we
Glimpse the always receding
True proposal in the glass

And join the horses, who dance,
Tremors of exactitude
Flaring, still fresh on their limbs.

from *In the Absence of Horses* (1983)

✥ Ana Halach Dodeach

From my mountain of words I can see
You on your mountain. Here is the plain
Between them, the text to be sponsored

By the bounding turf over which come
Tangible horses, tangible texts—
Here! For your eyes their rhythmical feet

Draw the text out in the marginal airs
From your mountain to mountainous cries
Of the man who wants to live in love,

Bear fruit in his hands, in a garden
To hear the ultimate song: *Where has
Your lover gone, beautiful among*

Women? I have said he has the eyes
Of doves. *Where, o fair one, does he feed?*
He feedeth among lilies. *Where, fair*

Among women, does he feed? He feeds
At Table With Fruit, Evening With
Roses, he feeds in the valley of

The text of songs, song for Solomon,
In spicy beds over which I watch.
With my mountain of words I see Him.

With his mountain of words I am seen.

❧ Passing Over Your Virtues

To pass over in silence
Is to acknowledge logic,
The necessity of form,

The stunning curve of language,
The curious way it seems
To turn out that "love" means "need"

Even in a lush garden.
To pass over the Red Sea
Or your bounty—so long as

True silence and not some tense
Paralysis of the false
Is achieved—then Passover

Is always a charity,
The painted fish in the blue
Water turns to their own colors.

To pass over in silence
Is to acknowledge you if
This chatter dissolve as it

Will in the marvelous sky.

❧ Coast and Walrus

I

Everything is larger than we can
Say, so we hardly notice the
Hazardous cliff behind us that falls

Slowly, in bits, down toward the lifeguard
At whose feet the swollen walrus bobs
In disregard for the lively child

And of us. We came for something else,
Me to live by you as though death
Had no dominion, you as though no

Fear of death had power to lounge
Behind you and lean uneasily
Against the continent. The smell stings

Like bees in the back of my skull. Here,
With nothing before the greedy eye
But rolling brine, faced with this vast, this

Uninterpretable cynosure,
We know how much we take on the faith
Of the tongue. Japan, for example,

And the restaurant beyond the cliff.
We pace the beach toward home and I can't
Speak in the thick air, so trail behind

You, embarrassed out of my creature.
Nothing speaks up from the sealed off surf.
Douleur is mute. Is pain of muteness.

II

The tide slumps down the beach, the walrus
Trails behind us as though some question
Shimmered to be answered, a question

The sea refuses, the sea shuts her mouth,
Lets a grumble depart from her chest,
Steadily noses Walrus along,

Right behind, and a giant poem
Struggles, just there, in the ocean,
Who has closed her throat, won't speak the flash

Of the dolphins, nor all of the times
I've said that to live within an arc
That graceful would be to live in love.

How without mistake they selected
Their waves and rode them! At first we
Mistook them for sharks. Then, we saw. They leapt.

Our eyes are full. It's a beginning,
Even if they take no custody
Of Walrus. I think of taking up

Your hand and the wind is, *tout d'un coup,*
Clean and sharp. I reel under the blow
But my skin rises to it, rises

Like feathers, and I answer the sea
With scrupulous divinities, my
Syllables reach yours, your skin rises.

✲ Truth on the Beach

Truth wears so many guises
And is garrulous, babbles
Deep in the waters of books,

Shakes loose from our skin and flies
While the bright waves break, just
In from Japan, is a matter

Of time between here and there—
California and Japan—
Time between the two of us,

All of the others, restless,
Each on an end of time that
Packs us, each immobilized

By the guises of truth but
There is just one thing takes
The guises of light and light is

Everywhere. We swim in it,
Simultaneous pinpoints
Irrevocably uttered

At the surprised face of Truth
Who gathers her skirts and swirls
In fury, brilliant at last.

Postcards from Jerusalem

I. First Impressions

Olive trees grow near Jerusalem,
Branching in the supple valley,
Offering penitent wood and fruit
For the crushing, oil for the light.
But I never learned Hebrew, never
Studied the small arts with which olives
Are carved out edible from the brine.
The hills seem salt-soaked, the blank rubble
To wait for something. A true weeping?

II. Missing You

Any glimmer alerted me and you
Were alert to any benign wind.
I would lean into your welcoming
Breath. The sky would gaze back and buoyant
Adonis, resurrected in blue,
Has been a brilliant pulse strolling with
No grief through my veins. Does this city
Remember your eyes? Jerusalem
Is built of bright, sensuous stone.

III. In the Beginning Was the Word

"Jerusalem, alias living
Donkeys, are plentiful . . ." *Daily News,*
1878, September
16. "Jerusalem ponies are
In high requisition." "[She] at last
Thought of trying her Jerusalem
Pony in the streets." Etc.
"Jerusalem letters: letters or
Symbols tattooed on the arms, body."

IV. Sights in the Old City: The Shops

The architecture of His eyes? The stone.
Weightless but hard olivewood carvings.
Prophets. Donkeys. Crosses. Pretty, but
No one piece suffices. I don't buy.
I never studied Hebrew but in
These streets the syllables rattle on.
The stones stand up well to the stagger
Of donkey hooves, the lion roars after
His prey, seeking his rough meat from God.

V. Sights in the Old City: The Horse

By the Western Wall a flesh-and-blood
Police horse jigs without certainty,
Thin but not truly haggard, perhaps
He gets some grain. The rider prevents
The approach of poetry as well
He ought—a timid pace prevents
Lameness. I like this horse who suffers
The city with nervous elegance.

VI. The Old City: Near the Via Dolorosa

On stone the horse seeks his elegance,
The lion and the stray cats their prey.
You can't fool a tourist, though—the gold
Is in the jewelry shops. The walls are

Made of stone, the horses of ignorance.
Olivewood toys. Some decent whiskey
Might revive my interest; I go
Hopefully seeking. God and I sit
In a cafe by the wide sepulchre.

VII. A Chosen People

I am alert to light but you are
Not here, so it is God and I who
Watch a group of Israeli soldiers
Tease an Arab vendor. Their guns swing
With their supple young movements as they
Walk away laughing, calling out,
"Suffer!" "'Bye!" *Why do they speak English?*
Why are they so lovely? Who are they?
All God's children. I leave them to God.

VIII. A New Coming

If you were to sit here beside me
And before us were to march donkeys
Carrying New Jerusalem past
As though it were wisdom, we would merge
With God, filled with the laughter of God,
Filled with light and the inhabitants,
Accustomed though they are to holy
Rubble, would live from that moment on
With their eyes bare with astonishment.

IX. A Tour of the Via Dolorosa

Alone in Jerusalem I am
Led by a child whose adequate French
Is soft on the Chemin de la Croix.
The child suppresses Arabic, I
Suppress English, and our voices meet
Like clean serpents coiled among the stones.
The horse passes again, his cadence
Foreign and bright, light without art like
Our syllables uselessly nimble.

X. The City's Endurance

No vow of ours can exclude journeys
Or eternal urban visions that
Emerge from historical leavings.
With what vow could we surround the Old
City's structure? Toy crosses? A dance?
If we danced all day long, all the way
From Jaffa Gate to Damascus Gate,
We would limp home. Without you I
Lean into the liquor of God's breath.

XI. A Note on Prophecy

But I collect no information,
Really, in this unrelieved brilliance,
Even though I walk with a people
Whose prayers have the form of factual
Utterance and whose prophets still dream
In a journalism beyond time:
Here, simply, is the certainty of light
And a thousand and one tales
Told of the fathers and their dancing.

XII. Trip to Bethlehem

All of dark humanity seems a
Heavy stagger in the blanket of
God's winey breath and horses, dancing,
Beasts of half-articulate rhythms.
I can't tell God from the domestic
Shocks of life on the stones. Foreigners
Should save their dancing for home and God
Will follow. The circle we draw around the
Sacred star creates the profane life.

XIII. The New City: The Cave of Destruction

The *idea* of such a monument,
With no song guaranteed to call us
Out again. Its sole inhabitant

Crouches in the shadows cast by soap
And candles, taunting us with the filth,
Mocking me with my fool bliss. I see
Just in time how the filth excludes you,
Even though you have a body, eyes
That wince away from cave and clutter.

XIV. The Wailing Wall

The light of Jerusalem is found
Out in Raphael, it is as though
The stones traded light the way our skins
Trade infrared, and while the soldiers
Pace before the wall, over the stones
They love, my skin moves with a soft jolt
Again. The light on the stones is not
About you. Now, to remember this
Wall of gold is to remember you.

XV. Leaving for Lod

Imagined grief and ecstasy's what
Built these magnificent walls and streets
Of stone. The real thing has worn them smooth.
He was His own architect but we
Submit to the vision of a bore
With an eye for the actual. So,
Farewell to gold, olivewood visions,
The dancing of divinities. Time
To leave this prophesy-stricken town.

The Claim of Speech

for Stanley Cavell

I

Must we mean what we say? Stick to it,
Be bound to, chained up beside the house,

Teased by boys on bicycles, fireflies,
The seasons as they pass out of reach?

We could try meaning nothing, a way
Favored in the brightest corridors

By those who pass from life to death through
Halls of learning and replace marriage

With justice. To mean nothing is to
Have nothing at heart, to be chained up

To the right of and a bit behind
The body: without marriage, justice

Prevails as the clenched hand of culture
On the most brutal bridle prevails

Against the motion beneath that wants
To claim the hand of culture. Against

The Horse in the horse, the Rider in
The rider, the heart beneath the tongue.

II

In the anarchies of the sensuous
Hands the order of love is leaping.

In a far corner of the landscape
A lover's hands leap in the skin's light,

And heroes' hands lap like tongues on necks
Curved with significance. The horses

Stamp and whinny, hint of caprioles
As urgently as our mute souls

And it is impossible to mean
Anything but motion. A dispatch

From the graceful landscape will arrive:
"He must be told." Lovers will obey

Thus leaving terror and time alone
To fend for themselves. I will obey,

Am obeying now, making poems
From chains, leaving the season alone—

You must be told (already your horse
Leaps beneath you!) *what you meant to say.*

On R. L. S. and Happiness

also for Stanley Cavell

I

The fate of women is still to dream
That he returns. Dreams of the husband
Are better than dreams of the rapist

In that there is a moment of joy
Before the breakup, when the mind moves
Truculently off from the body

To make coffee. It is impossible
In either case to dream of murder,
Impossible to dream of nothing

But the moment of the dream itself
Whatever happens in the daytime.
I have a flag and lead my armies

To knowledge. I admire the flowers
Smeared golden over all my meadows.
I study Apollo. Still you toss

In your dream of Phaeton rising
Again, while in my dreams you are you,
Merely. I have no other report.

II

Although, "My heart rouses / thinking to
Bring you news / of something that concerns
You / and concerns many men. Look at . . . ."

III

I know the motions of the horses—
The motions of faith—and it is time
That I insist, even though the Jew

Couldn't prove he was human. Neither
Can you. I can't prove the horse, but here
Is your pain anyway, and here are

Instructions against it. It's a salt.
Consider the ocean. Consider
The infinite fishes, how they swim.

Consider us at the shore, weeping
To show our sympathy with water.
It's not enough. Only in the most

Careful details of the most extreme
Philosophies, the most careful stones
Of the breathless cathedrals, the claims

Of the most elaborate musics
On our souls do we start to dissolve
As though we had a home, and lived there.

✻ Our Condition at Twilight

At twilight our abandoned symbols
Rustle where we dropped them earlier.

Leaves that gleamed as though brilliant with our
Views of them and all our intentions—

Our plans, made in the morning, to learn
The symbolism of tulip trees—

Rattle with only our first inspired
Guesses for meaning. The wind itself

Comes to spread the mess and thus to retard
The clean rhetoric of the leaves, blur

The intent focus of the sun that flashed
On the leaves as though the sun were the

Idea. The contrasting night with
No vision in it dampens even

The whispers of what we might have known
Until we can't tell if failure is

Of us, or merely the failure of
The light. The light! That clarified

All it touched? Or chose, somehow, to touch
Only that which was already blessed

With its own insignificant clear
Edges? The leaves, for instance, edged with

Catching and radiating filaments
That held light like meaning on the lawn

And tossed it ably through the window
Onto the dim couch where we will

Rest, our forms still round, and damper than
Leaves. For now, before the dew thickens,

Our condition is this: We can hear
The leaves, blown into corners, just out

Of sight, and can just make out our forms.
I can recall that your shirt was blue

All morning and afternoon, and that
During the same period the fine

Botticelli print seemed, by means of
Its colors to be a means of truth.

The secret fluids that keep us round
In our forms will dominate the dark

As though they shone in their passageways
Luminous behind our closed eyelids.

Our condition at twilight is the
Condition of meaning as itself

A condition. The memory light
Leaves us, the knowledge that once there

Was light is the condition we find
Ourselves in when the knowledge that once

There was darkness begins to fade out.
Here we are: intimate in the dark

Where only the willful idea
We were born from, and born to, will stay

Us in our journey through the velvet
Stillness in which we will understand

That the truth is before light and
After the light and ever more will be.

🌿 In the Absence of Horses

I. All For Love

Action is love. Once stillness
Is lost, once the surface blurs
And the lake heaves with a stone
In its heart, action failing
Is love choking and stillness

Becomes a putrefaction.
Small pulses of the murky
Water, meaningless algae,
Have force to blind the fishes
Until they leap through the air
Complete acts of silver said
In silver.
                Action is speech
(Not speech action) the utter
Parole, its benevolence
A fusion. When focus and
Motion swiften to a brief
Rendezvous, action is love
And love's the only action.

The rest is the departure
Of stillness, the glass ruined,
The lake incoherently
Shuddering

Throat and mouth shuddering can
Acknowledge nothing, something
Else comes out. To acknowledge
This is to recite, sometimes
To speak as though there were that
Obedience in our words.

II. Recital

       Because the right and wrong
Appeared, the Way was injured,
Because the Way was injured,

Love became complete.
             There is
Such a thing as completion
And injury,
        such a thing
           also
  as no completion
And no injury. We may
Love, or speak, or until
Death abstain from completion.

Something has been said. With our
Words we form recitals. In
Our recitals we stand forth,
Heirs apparent to the world.

III. Argument with Samuel Daniel

". . . not the contexture of words
But the effects of action
That gives glory to the times"

But the contexture of words
Is action

IV. *Courage,* Cry the Inmates

Now hurt speaks its circular
Language. Spasmodic, obsessed
With origins the tongue of
Damage thrusts acrobatic

Syllables up its own ass,
Holed up in the certainty
Of imprisonment. I mean

Ordinary damages:
"My finger hurts," or, "He left
Again," or, "My father is
Still trying to murder me."
Such damage is hard to speak
Of, but speaks anyway, so
Plain are our appeasements and
Black.
But we make our decisions

About who speaks and in what
Fading or expanding light
The speakers stand. We can say,
Let us go to the park and
Stand upon the ground awhile
Until we come up at last
With something totally new and
True to say.
                        Damage speaks
In circles, but the human,

Speaking of and from all his
Hot hurts, can speak up, move up
And out, finally, not out
Of damage, but out of the
Darkness of thought, its bondage
To the facts.

Merely naming the facts leaves
Them behind: Speech gestures at
What we were and rises thus
To a universe beyond
Speech. Once beyond speech we find

There is an action of speech
At the center of all our
Acknowledgments and we are
Ourselves after all, damaged,
Brutal, and speaking, brutal
And pure.

V. More on the Question of Anguish

On whether in the poem's
Flesh a grain of sand, fester
Of foreign object, foreign

Pain. Whether to heal, embrace,
Press softly, is to suck out
Bitter brightness of language,

Relieving that pressure. Whether
The Beloved's dewy breath
Eases completely the song's

Heart, refreshes the desert
Until we live without words
In an evening of roses—

Or there is less, beginning
As a query about the rose,
Single and distant, clearly

Nothing but a rose and truth
The desire for roses when
The desert is black with light.

Whether or not one action is
A rose or the glitter eyes
Take on in the desperate

Parchment of these violent
Sands that shift, grumbling, and toss
Miracles of intention

Up before our eyes. But such
Questions may not be answered:
Here, in the grass, are horses.

VI. Digression

A fish, ascending, affirms
Gravity: Head and tail point,
Plunging, to the earth, actions

Are made by their syntax, the
World is made available
In the syntax of a fish.

The fish, like a syllable or
A real poet, inherits
The earth and in one motion
Gives it away.
                    Desperate
Movement is not an action:

A horse stumbles along. Edge
Of a leaf rots in the grey
Wind. A man, telling a lie,
Breathes on the mirror, disturbs
The surface.
                    In the fogged glass
A child or an artist will
Trace the liar's name, tracing
Pardon for horse, leaf, life.

VII. Beyond Fishes: Mare and Foal

Here in the grass, are horses.

When the foal lay curved, brooding
In the dark mare, his feet fringed,
Softened, action was stillness,
Stillness the only action,

Until she broke sweatily
In the ignorance that cries
Out of itself. Now their heads turn,
Each toward each other, the mare's
Head and heart dance, the foal's head
Dances this way and that way—
Becoming actions in that
Symmetry. What becomes them

Is that each horse is dancing
Within and surrounded by
The other's eyes: Now their hooves!
Blaze into definition.
They surround the light, outlined
Against the clear wind, knowing
What they mean. See how the heart,
Defined in its lake of blood,
Turns this way and that, rising
To show ever new facets
Of damage. Consider the mind,
Turning in the congealed air
To catch each dancing facet
Until it can contemplate
The whole heart in its motion
And make it whole. The pale foal

Stumbles in the wind, numb in
The wind until he dances
Between the mare's gaze and ours
For wholeness. He eats boldly,
Bruising the grass, and the grass
Shines in the wake of his teeth.

VIII. "That,"

Fish and lake shine in the wake
Of the dance, teaching us that
The past is gone, is become
The past; terms for the snows
Of *l'antan;* meaning's the first
And last valor of language.

Our delicate studies of
The hidden parameters,
Spaces in equations for
Unpronounceable details
That slosh along without us,
Yield the information that
The present of love is an
Act, an utterance swift and
Prompt. The present sky holds back

Blue in a saucer. The lake
Reflects without knowing
Refractory spectrums. So,

IX. In the Absence of Horses

Our study is poetry,
Is the art of the horseman
In whose gaze the world dances,
The art of the mind finding
The heart turning in the press
Of the mind. The horse enters
The turn of the heart. The heart
Enters the turn of the poem.

Higher thoughts than these exist
And higher questions edged with
Silver, but find no higher
Answers lest you turn your clear
Horseman's gaze from the dancing
World and leave the foal crumpled
In a hot shadow. The act

That broke the surface beneath which
The unpronounceable still
Sloshes breaks open ever
More brilliant surfaces. To
Say the eyes may lay their claim
To any more than this, to
Some orange interior, some
Heart of Africa, some
Flaming core of dark truth, is
To dissect the optic nerve,
Leave the mind to move blindly
From inference to brutal
Inference. The brow's clear lines
Inferred from the nether shapes
Are not instructions, reason
As you will of horses, so
Careless on their hoofy legs.

In the absence of horses
The Beloved will suffice
And will change on the brutal
Turns of the tongue, becoming
The Betrayer, betrayed, and
Hollow figure of fullness
For seventeen years until
At last lovers, abandoned

Again to their gazing are
Figures of knowledge, figures
Of action for which any
Steady emblem is enough
And any time, time enough

For the world opens gently
With the song in its embrace.

❧ Night Track

I

We had ideas, the dogs had ideas, and the world
shouldered abruptly away like a rabbi
on Christmas Eve. We were
lonely hunters praying to the caverns
of hounds, knowledge in their flews, the night
swift and black.
                    Lonely hunters?

the summer settled and
rose again delicately
lapping at my breasts

but there was a wind problem, the dogs
leaping into the wind, we followed: god
in a field of god leaping into god's breath found

a lost child, a rabbit, a criminal, empty burrows

(god)

the dogs closing the gap and no
fictions in that field, that
summer we were to have been in love
but closed the gap instead and lived
in the crystal wind, not
for the quarry

found god anyway

turned from your breath, turned from my breath,
gulped the fleshless air,
turned from your loins, from that story
no womb-fruit, no fictions, god

in a field of god, no study
of our seasonal graces, recited the wind

not in our sleep
                    we turned in pure
focus, unblanketed in the shifting stars, steady
at the center of the dark wind

II

The thing we liked about tracking
was not daring to make mistakes: *hound's*
gotta hold that line, run that fox
all the still night, no noise, no lullabies

no stopping for logic
                        just one music and *the logic*
of the inheritance that put that bugle
in the hound bitch's throat, angels
and the scents oracular

at the end of the run quiet
hands, silken ears, our flesh
become a brilliant nocturnal creature
in which we would live forever

and still do. Morning
slumps at our ankles. We live on,
restless at the end of the run.

Toward a Cultural History

We made the ones who trot, backs
Flawless and bare to the wind.
In that wind evenness of stride
Was a theological
Elegance. We drew the loins
Long on the high descendants
Of Sham and ploughed supple turfs
Before their hooves that they might
Reach infinitely to a

Significance of thundering.
We prayed for the gathering
Of hooves into corners tighter
Than the panic of cattle

And still the horses dodged us
Like fireflies. We prayed to their
Refined bones, built palaces
For horses, horses around
Palaces of certainty,
Nations around palaces,
Gardens around bleak pastures

And forbade the bitter wire
For the fences, and weeping.

Now the grooms and the women
Kneel at the ragged center
To study pathology,
Alone with the actual.
The names of the bones betray
The grounds, the architecture,
The king whose insomnia
Is a state secret. Within
Their hooves inflamed coffin bones
Swell rebelliously and burst
Through their soles, lie on the world's
Surface, glowing like our hearts.

An Historical Note: Staghounds

Early in the time of the griffon's
Actual existence, we crafted
An odd holiness. There were whelped long
Hounds, with a vision that could love the
Shy, subtle motions of light left by
Deer in those forests of softening
Horizons. Searching by deerlight, hounds

Lengthened into the branching calmness
Where nothing at all was owned except
By knowledge (as of the plans smaller
Creatures made in the civil mosses).

In a forest made lucid by deer.
As if leaves were a plan for a text
Illuminated by feral monks
Who would keep their vows even though the
Light might harden against them. In that
Wide forest text hounds stopped reading
The paranoid old wolvish custom
Of huddling in dens. How kindly they
Bounded, predators as always but

Now with what dreamy, elegant strides!

The Moral for Us

Never trust servants, that's the
Shabby moral King Midas
Kept with him and earnestly
Told the curious poet
Who came with ulterior
Motives. And whispers of this?
The benevolent donkeys
Still graze, tossing furry ears.
Silver winds whistle through each
Ear, and ear of corn, and head
Of wheat and shimmering blade
Of grass. We listen, leaning
Forward over our yellowed
Copies as though they told us
Holy secrets and not the
Feeble gossip of poets—
Some noble new truth. Gossip
Will endanger no furtive

Listeners. Let us eavesdrop,
Rather, on the perilous
Dreams of royalty who in
Their sleep turn visions to gold.

Gaugin's White Horse

There he stood, quite suddenly,
Innocent nose to foreleg,
Bent against no betrayal,

As though all the gods had laps
And were not inflamed. Shadows
Bore fruit. Edible mosses

Exhaled an eternity
Of breath. Someone asks whether
Gaugin held his when this horse

Flowed out into the foreground
Like an ethics of texture.
Now, it matters. We, with our

Breath as heavy, as rapid
As paint, reach to pluck the horse,
Letting time back in, and take

Flesh for the trope of the horse,
The horse for a trope of grace,
Perception in place of the

Acts of the heart, for granted.
It was all actual. Here,
The emptied frame has become

What fills in for the prior
Question—not the one about
Wanting our innocence back,

Or how to send it forward,
A wisdom of matted manes,
Nor where the laps of the gods

Fall to when the sun rises.
The question is behind mouths
And won't come out of the frame

As long as we keep choking.
Ease in your throat is what lets
The head of the white horse swing

Downward through air, toward water.
Ours are the mouths Gaugin's brush
Bends to, compelled to answer.

Canvas with a Bit of Tyger Showing

Without myth? Without emblem?

They prowled, then, in the first trance,
Neither noble nor debased.
Theirs was the trance of attack,

The trance of eros inflamed,
And the trance of predation.
So what was dark, original,

Prior to the need for truth,
Was bred in the tyger trance
Of analysis. Bred there

In a heart fully exposed
To a light it owned alone.
They happened before crime did,

Their forms occurring under leaves
That guarded them from wisdom.
There was one intent upon

A shaft of sun. The only
Right thing for you and me to
Say, was: Stay out of the light!

It had to be said softly
Or the attention of the
Brighter tygers would enclose

Us immediately. This
Was no performance, no sign
Linking boundaries, no tie

Between souls. We were either
In their light and therefore not
In our own, or we stayed back

On the fruitful plain among
The placid enquiries of
Courteous hooves, devising

Speculations on the leaves
Through which the light of tygers
Filtered. It was not for us.

Or, if it was, that meant no
More of the plain, the hooves, the text
We made of leaves. No more cat

In the corner before which
Pranced the horses in *haute école*.
Art had to do with keeping

Cats off, with building the halls
In which real horses danced their
True revelations of form.

We put the matter aside,
Focussed on the drum of love.
It takes awe before hooves,

A feel for the domestic
Pussy and a new terror
Of the facts before we learn

To paint hoof and paw without
Leaving one or the other
To savage intimacies.

❧ Ierushalayim Shel Zahav

for Colleen Lerman

All of my lovers dance in your hands
getting it right at last as your skin
seeks me out and is brighter
in my chambers than the creatures
with sharp feet and soft eyes

and once in a while we are lucky
find a hill that is steep enough

our feet become real in the ascent
the path is wide enough for both of us

because we are not goats we sometimes
need to know that we are not goats
our only nimbleness that of waiting,
endurance, you said, and perhaps it's true, but

In Jerusalem I met a man who gave silver
away to thieves. Later, in California, a poet
read her poem of the feet of dinosaurs
uttered in the golden hills, informing us
and today my daughter moves quietly into prophecy,

a flame in the house, says, "That was our friend Motke
who gave silver to thieves, who found
the footprints." They said he could give silver
to thieves, and he did, and Jerusalem
glitters on her hills in that light, and Motke
dances there, I think, for how else
could he *see*? And somewhere there are thirty Jews
with sharp feet and soft eyes. The trouble
with the hill is not that it is empty of deer
but that it overflows with meaning
wherever we put our feet. The hill—I mean,
Jerusalem, what lies outside the world
and is the value of the world. There is no escape
from the gleaming hills of the city.
Its inhabitants cannot sin it away. Some of them
see this, and today my daughter glances
at the poems of the American poet. They are not
for her, but even as she lays the book down
in the wrong place the city inspires her breath
with the gold that gushes from the hill
when the creature bruises its surface. Look, I mean
that the children of the Arabs are torn,
torn, are less than the food of wolves, that
every pilot is an archangel; we cannot
turn from them while their relentless planes
surround the sun, and, true form to their forms
murder comes after the lines in the poem
where all of my lovers dance in your hands
getting it right at last, that you
and you, and you, whoever you are
still seek me out and will remain brighter,
brighter. And somewhere there are those thirty
Jews, and the song will end on a hill
where nothing will dim its nimbleness

from *The Parts of Light* (1994)

Between Fences

for John Hollander

And then discussed with the horse
The attributes of God, made
Peace with them. This was called

Pace between fences, was judged
For balance on turns, because
The flying changes, treasured

From the start, had been marked out
As one excellence against
The gruffer idolatries.

The horse was civil but liked
To discuss God and still does,
Changing leads from right to left,

Engaging fully the stout
Haunches. The change is analyzed
As shifts in the count of hooves, is

No optical illusion:
What we cannot see is not
There to be seen but the ground

Keeps the pace between fences
Steady until the new fence
Looms up; reason arches

Firmer than all our prayers, and takes charge.

Touch of Class
or
View from Within Any
Imperial Riding Academy

In these mere scenes and landscapes
Dilettantes prefer, what blurs is

Becoming as truth entranced,
Formed before No and Yes, before

The choice between opulence
And laughter. In this mare's leaps

We count the ripples spreading
From God's joy that this mare's legs

Make ripples no matter who
Understands landscapes. The hooves

Of horses touch the spellbound
Throats of new constellations:

They shine with benevolence
As if nature thought about

How geometry loves us.

The New Hound Puppy

Now it is time for her name—

Start the call. The time may come
For her job, which is to run
Holes in the palpable wind

Hallowed by world and the world
Will collapse, follow this hound
Through meteoric valleys,

Wolf-shag domains. Here God says
Himself through the wolf until
A slenderness of hound bitch

With a speed like silk shimmers
At God, all arc and angle,
Revelation for voice. So

It was in the beginning
And evermore shall be, so
Her arcs speak back to the light

Which is become an affair
Of luminous shadows, so
It was in the beginning

And evermore shall be in
Her temporal impudence,
Intended as litany.

The Figure 1

```
Consider: You and I and the others and Euclid because
the perfect is so hot in us failing to see it below
profane trisections I mean we inherit this sacred
theorem, true, but NOT from that high priest of
ruler and compass FINAL questions seem to cry
from the past If CODINGS of answers without
reverence yield IMPERFECT theories flawed
methods may be INVOCATIONS nevertheless
This chanting WILL SAVE YOU in all of
your visions Behold above the equal
within the inequalities of a mind
that was given after all that I
or that you may see Knowing a
rule is not seeing the form
The restless imbalancings
of the many are our joy
for see from despised
triads inexactness'
very heart arrive
harbingers only
but true ones
of the Form
O at last
to have
about
one
1
```

Morley's Theorem: The three points of intersection of the adjacent trisectors of any triangle form an equilateral triangle

❧ The Dog and the Word

The catechism of dogs
is to attack
at a word, laugh

at another, so
it has been written
so consider

the flash of a Golden
Retriever, mouth so swift
on the pheasant, prairie

chicken, stick or ball, bit
of twine, so
tender, this divine

seizure that wants nothing more
for itself, stands
to deliver and reveals

in the bird dog's celebrant
profile the sky
to the naked eye. Grab

without greed, we
have no noun
for it, only

the one command.

✻ Some General Principles of the Art of Riding

I

First to consider are cadence, suppleness,
The lightness of great skill
Which is control, which
Disappears into
         ease:

This requires great labor of preparation
And cannot be sought,
It must be waited for

   Thus the way to ride at spread fences is to create
         impulsion   impulsion

Not speed and
         wait
       don't panic
       this is the hardest thing
               HOW

Do you stay with a pony that can just about
              jump out
                   of his skin?
     sound skills
       pretty chilly
         little moves
           let him do his thing

Look at Mary Chapot, tough to beat
With natural tact on White Lightning
      splitting the difference
        winning the cup

II

The novice stands before a balance of masters
Properly abject but not bowed, the head must be up
Not to repeat errors of technique, thus

    We are grateful
      (all of you)

        to Colonel D'Endrody

        writing his thesis while captive
        at the foot of the Caucasus Mountains
        on the shore of the Black Sea
        where he did no riding

Grisone wrote well but he is deplored
For heavy hands, rigid control
From which the horse soon escapes back
                    into
                    your
              lap,
                    Grisone used
              elaborate bits, numerous tricks
              that have no place in the
                          ART

III

Yes, there are devices which can be used
                with great caution
            by a Rider

Who has learned to evaluate the importance of various
                          MOVEMENTS
By "feeling"
            this is a delicate matter
Not beginning
When a pupil knows one trot from the other by clues
Or can count the feet, striking to canter:

The student stands
At the threshold of art
when compelled
By the true stride of every horse
he happens to find is his mount.

V

Paris:
Pessoa on Gran Geste
A genuine artist, sophisticated,
Cerebral, memorably
Revealing his supple elegance

Tempting us to take foolish chances

Most of us should remain absolutely quiet in the air
flight
Is largely a gift from the horse

V

Notice Steinkraus
Proving to Europeans in their own saddles that Americans
Still transcend and ride

He warns
that at crucial moments when
forward movement on a line
or turn
is lost
it is
a great mistake we all make to want to pay
attention to the
head when
the real solution
lies in summoning
the liveliness
that comes from the rear

✗ Riding Skills

They say you never forget
So you had sure better not
But you do. The light chuckles

To hear this, chuckles out loud
As you pick up your courage
With the reins. That's what happens

When you pick up the reins, legs
Better remember! because
Riding is remembering

To ask politely. The horse
May tell you her stable name,
Then the one she dances by,

Or may not, but if she does
The light stops its mocking,
Gets going on the smooth streets

Of the world. The horse's scope,
The confident cathedrals,
Allow truth its say as if

Riding were remembering.

✣ A Point of Technique

When ease comes the classic horse's hooves
Roughen the ground so in their spring hard
Prayers that for a moment everything

Is visible; words lie all before
The relaxed landscape. Cramped up to peer
Through the miracles of landscape we see

Instead and become the patina
Of the holy cities as blood widens
Like love, especially in Hebrew . . .

Truth is like that when for brief moments
At a time we see forever and
The light at last is good for nothing

From the need-bound darkness, from the long
Stumble of the horses over all
In an instant in the startled air.

When death comes horses are not like this.
Their heads lengthen, their teeth from calling
Form rectangular swirls as the fall

Of the air tears, gives their teeth away.

✣ Girl on a Lawn

The head of the mongoloid child bobs
On its stalk; the sun

Is nearly that graceful, that
Splendid. The child considers

Ways to move across the lawn. Jonquils
On her brilliant path stand

Before her and she moves to
Step elsewhere but moves

Through them instead like speech
Lurching. Speech moves headlong

Through our throats and language
Is as lovely as a child, we are

As mindless as jonquils, the sun
Is nearly that graceful.

Grasshoppers

Children cup their hands
over them and hold

keenly still against
the plump and

Pop
of their flight. It matters

to let go
quickly for the rhythm

of the thing, capture
and grasping are

release as
with thought

such as grasshoppers
think of poignant

accuracy of angles
against the palms, the grass

or the word against
the concave of the throat.

❧ On the Grounds of the Statewide Air Pollution Research Center

seeing a rabbit
I ached into each
detail brown
and gray
and white fur, red
vital veins in
translucent ears, we

stayed still
rabbit and I
stopped by the
sun and air but

when I reached
for my pen
to write it

rabbit scurried
away shuddering
the bushes

❧ Balance at the Halt

The horse is the largest animal
of love so

is the bluebird
                and the logician
who did not doubt stones may
have been kind to them
for all he knew. This shows up

in the way words
face into infinity when they do, finding
the other in the vast gleam
of exteriority and it is
a brave affair like the blemished badge
of justice that does not protect the heart even

as the horse holds his stand and the cop
while the contraband air riots.

                Or I could say that truth halts
at road signs, right or wrong. Horsemen
speak of balance at the halt; knowledge picks
through the wood crowded with the glitter and glitz,
gigantic, of all knowledge is not and must learn
balance at the halt which is a matter
of motion because horses as they instruct spook

first and answer questions
later knowing themselves
as generous surfaces.

                The section of the old army manual
about traversing the minefield said to drop the reins,
give your horse his head and that's one map
of know-how: True pace

is the collected extension
from which beauty flies everywhere as your mount settles
in the poise of self carriage.

What Transpires

When it transpired that the meaning
Drifting in the limbs of the young dog was
Eclipsable, like any old light, some
Learned a new
Name for God, some garbled
Older inscriptions already worn

By the softness of wringing
Words, hands, notes, cries into crevices
In place of significance.
                              Trapped in infinite
Light we cannot pronounce
Its name, but Goethe,
Dying, could.

Dogs do dance. Not a trick of the light but
The light. What is left over
Vanishes like our helplessness
As when the gazelles after a last flash
Disappear before we can trace
On air the shapes of our mouths
We take for explanation.

❧ The Young Airedale

On moonlit snow the young dog,
Airedale, bred like a furnace,
Makes fantasy strides, his legs

Wide in profile, a pre-Muybridge
Hound in a poem such as
Anyone was permitted

To write, once. This one is fast.
His breeder says he is splendid,
That she isn't sure she dares

Breed another this superb.
His movement so swift and black
He casts a shadow paler

Than he is. Leaps free of it
Tonight and when he pauses
Among other blacknesses,

Crackles of branches and leaves
Left over from last season's
Hurricane, I know easily

Where he is, where the blackness
Is warm, like holes in the ice
Through which spirit fish carol.

The Runner and the Mountain

Why he wanted the mountain? What in
The ground failed to support the right airs
Above ground? On he runs, and as he

Runs his footsteps shatter the sand's crust
And remain where they are. Behind him
And before him the laws of form fall,

Fall. The mountain retreats, big and gay
In a remote diction of gesture,
Diction of a space that figures forth

Hyperboles of separation—
The mountain's vehement expression
Of gaps no stride can measure. He reads

This, reads in the delicate air want
Of mountains and runs on, a gnostic
In the ignorant wilderness until

His foot lands square on time, then hovers
Where bare Elements meet the singing
Shell of prophesy and there embrace,

Figuring forth possible mountains
Of form. He is taken up, caressed,
Enclosed within the mountain's pleasure.

❧ The Parts of Light

During the dark of the moon
(Now, as you nod at your book
In lamplight) a sober-winged owl

Eyes the moon as both remain
Out of sight. Thus moon and owl
Converse, keeping the ocean

Tides, moon and owl aloft there
As we, our eyes as high up
Over the book as need be, keep

The gods, like us, aloft. Our
Words on the wind wrap the world
In august conversations,

Human speaking intersects
The path to the void, the light
In its fractions, and the sun

And the sun's opposite star's
Mystery of water pours
Untidy, chilly knowledge

Out like a beneficence.

A Mosaic

. . . mais le vision de la justice est le plaisir
de Dieu seul.
—Rimbaud

No violence. Volunteer gazelles
Nude against leopards, and they all graze
On air, never waking from our dreams.

Now the mind is a museum. Thus:
Honor to the heart, encompassing
Grateful voles whose measureless gazing

Welcomes all seasons into the earth
Who comforts them after their sojourns.
We welcome the earth, immortal

And faithful as we are, despite death
In the valleys. Deliberately returning
Itself to us, the earth remains blind

To what we asked for in heedless youth,
Skipping to the warning on poems that
We keep these prayers from heat and flame

Lest the hunt begin its conflagrations
Of mind. Now we all live in rapture
And the loss of rapture replaces what

In the gazelle and the leopard,
The mosaics and the museum,
Prefigured grace: that slightest trembling

Of gaze that signaled what was other
Than the perfections of peace. Whence come
The perfections of war. Welcome

Of the earth is still our bitter joy
For there is no lord of hosts for us
(However gallant it is to hope)

Beyond the hope that this past, that sky,
This delicious beauty of a haunch
Or that power of springing up and

Beyond peace, this reach that can only guess
At the pleasure of God as young birds
Guess at air, their scabrous necks craning,

Their heads high, is what we want to be.

A Breed Standard for the Border Collie

Old Magic, useful to the farm, makes work
The eloquence of the place with no
Help from the weather, no high or low

Coutures of the peasant's drudgery—
Picturesque as low dress may be in
Our pricey galleries. Starvation

Is a drudgery Pip and Gael
Disdain. Failure is a drudgery
Too; what the collie—intent on what

Eloquence may be got from the sheep—
Desires, is that the proportions should
Matter to the farmer as collies

Find them, for there must be no farm thing
That is not eloquent, no farm thing
That is only that, no rag and fluff

Midden of kindness, no sugar clogged
Affections to excuse imbalance.
A dog with balance and style instructs

The sheep in this chastity for no
Reason beyond the collie's intent
Designs on the beasts, their pastures.

Later the collie takes up love and
Leaves it again to the imbalance
Of heartthrob, the invasionary

Conundrums, the tartish logics of loss.

All of My Beautiful Dogs Are Dying

My beautiful dogs are dying and
There are others as beautiful if
I am brave enough in my dotage

To face that beauty again, make it mine
In an authenticity of haunch,
Perfection of desire as of that

Young Brittany who, briefly, hunted
Birds and the very essence of bird,
Sharing with me the sky that had been

Able to intend bird, dog, woman,
Desire. Without the beautiful dogs
No one dares to attend to desire;

The sky retreats, will intend nothing,
Is a ceiling to rebuke the gaze,
Mock the poetry of knowledge.

My death is my last acquiescence;
Theirs is the sky's renunciation,
Proof that the world is a scattered shame

Littering the heavens. The new dogs
Start to arise, but the sky must go
Deeply dark before the stars appear.

Ion, Released from the Vows of Love, Replies to Socrates

I can only stand and look, my friend,
And tell the tale of Proteus
Again. The shapes you see when my gaze

Holds yours are you because Proteus
Is a mirror, time is a mirror,
You and I and the sun are mirrors.

The poet tells how a leopard sprang
From the eyes of desire; in this
We see the truth that will not make sense

For she loves us beyond our reasons
For inquiring, she replies to us
As the sea replies to the moon's long

Philosophies of motion. My craft
Lies in knowing this far too swiftly
To tell you. It is knowledge that weeps,

The diaspora of the goddess
Whose faith lives in our love of the sun,
Whose gray eyes regard us from the hill.

❧ Huck Finn, Credulous at the Circus

To be gulled, even in the afternoon
Of reason, into a belief
In the sudden access of sobriety

Conferred on the clown by the lithe voltes,
Mistaken caprioles of the liberty
Of horses—to be so gulled

Was to watch from the shadows,
Evading again the town as
Revealed in the burnt-black sun, and blink

In the glare of knowledge, in a light
Falsely thickened by scoundrels
Of revealing. The ringmaster, sharp

With artistry, unfolded his face
In the shape of logic and cleared up
The act and bowed. Who but the squinting

Vagrant boy would fear for the rider
When the rider leaped, when his head was in
The show, actual beneath the shift of hooves?

❧ Reasons Not to Own a Wolf-Dog

Because they are like smoke you
Look and they are not
Looking back but there is still

Smoke in the house and something
Is Wrong! There must not be smoke
In the house. In Virginia

There is Keesha, who slips off
Behind a tree out of reach
Of the heart. You feel your heart

As the hot awkward grab lunge
Sweaty in its palms that she
Says it is in her way of

Slipping away like smoke, but
Unlike smoke leaving behind
No stench, no consolation

Or what appears to console
And does, but only when sure
Evidence of fire, or at

Least heat as answer to
One's own heat, is like solace—
(A hushed pungent incense of

Acknowledgement? of love?) (Go
Try it! Cry: "Love!" to the place
She never was. She is gone)—

Or—remains, as wit remains
As the innocence of the farm
Grown intellectual for

Wit's sake and not for the filth
Of refusal. The horses,
The old tricolor collie,

Are safe—safe from the deftly
Charged light in the landscape's eyes,
Even the landscape's headlong
Joy beyond joy and even if
She slips past your heart she slips
Cleanly and leaves no damage.

Reasons not to own her are
Reasons to own her if you can
Own up to the quick impact

Of *Canis lupus* who is
Never inside except in
Immaculate chastity.

✣ Before the War

We ask aloud, knocking on God: Our last words—
will they be in a familiar language, one
that knows us as a sheepdog
knows her sheep, or at least like a dog with the flock and
against wolves, and just with it too, like Job
with his shepherds?

But that was all before the war
became so huge it overspilled Jerusalem,
all we could say about her and all
Job said too, besieged by men whose fathers
he would have "disdained
to set among the dogs of my flock!" and our friendship

Was all in what we said about the war
in those days, even before
it broke out, my dear, as though the war
were the wide world sweetened
with goat paths. One day

The deficiencies of speech grated
oh intolerable and the next day
or so the war swelled even further. We retreated
from our words, which was the way
life went on. Why there is no truth

In the throat of the mob, in the chorus, is
not clear, but your goats are quiet this morning, there
is not to be found truth
in the mob's throat. Here is truth:

Mark the keen grace of seagulls
staggered by swift gusts, how
only in that best of graces cold
is beaten back, mocked
as if by the purposeful slant
away of temporal wings. Power

Explodes thus and the eyes
flame with rapture; here is the hook
of justice, even in a flock, but there is falsehood
in the mob, the woman casualty
her body protesting with the chorus
just before it tumbled over the bridge, no
truth in the mob; this is a refutation

Of the excluded middleman. Truthless bodies, casual, not up to the
    world
and tumbling.
Stay home and listen
for the telephone on which you will hear
some truth, conference call or no, and when
time proves more interesting
than your heart seek philosophy
apart from the mob because Truth

with nothing to say for herself
hums along with the mob now like a voice
inventing variations

And the gods—oh Socrates!
        the gods
are unkind to each other and happiness
is the war ethic
that tried me and found me
wanting, as did pity. Hence: A rubble of broken fossils

trips travelers on their way home, sweepings
of what, withering in the valley, we failed to say, windy threads
that brought the mountains down. It is enough
to trip a goat, insouciant in the gayest season. Afterward

poetry is our only kindness
and all our joy when we are ready
to be named again, mistaken again
for the lion rampant with benevolence
at the stern gate.

✤ Listening Post

A brave man, sir. In 1968
He walked through a mine field.

You're not listening. I am
So listening. No,

You're not. This train
Goes through to Berlin and here

We are. Our horses will come later,
When there's time for that and they may
Carry us again on their buoyant backs. We will live,
Here on our side of the Berlin Wall, for horses
Have no interest in skeletons including
Those in the White House, look, Aristotle
Had a reason for writing the way he did, there are
Always the horses at stake. Someone
Must worry about the children's pony, that tough
Hearted little creature whose feet flame and kill him
At the drop of a can of grain. So that's
The job we keep not doing, and how many times
Do you think a pony can die and rise again? But
Don't forget to excuse yourself when you leave
The table to negotiate the long flight of stone stairs

Cut into the hillside. I am trying to say everything
At once because poetry is a hero, poetry
Is a war hero, you're not listening. I am
So listening. No, you're not. Yes, I am, those
Stairs, you're talking about the ones you have to climb
Down in order to get to the barn where the hay
Is stored, and you're warning me about not twisting my ankle
On my way to feed the horses, right? And you already told me
All about the manure ring, too slippery in the rain but:
Yes. When you put horses in such an area, tend them
Under an honest sun and they walk
About for years, sometimes galloping, sometimes even prancing
To our touch, the ground becomes flammable.

Yes. Yes. Yes, I am trying to say that the ground
Has become flammable.
                              Excuse me I have to go
Feed the horses. Don't forget the liniment
For Snowbound's bowed tendons, he's the one
Who will do it, from whose back the children
Will catch the brass ring, and they will do this
Whatever we do, but take care of Snowbound's legs
And take care of the children's pony.

In the play, it is an evil policeman in Prague
Who praises the hero. Someone must praise the hero.

St. Luke Painting the Virgin

St. Luke's eyes are steady on the babe.
I, insufficiently transfixed,
Am led inexorably beyond
Van der Weyden's (you call him Roger,
Just as you ought)—beyond the window
Roger has set behind radiant
St. Luke, peaceful knower, to gardens,
And beyond them

            to find in the clear
Distance the delicate city street
Where the figures of humanity
Consult the ground, their eyes helplessly
On the details of history that
Hold them there in the street as the laws
Of perspective, not imperfectly,
Hold the infant before the saint's eyes.

It is the beauty of these figures
As background, as reinterpreted
Landscape I cry for; to be landscape
Is not to be at the center, not
The first thing the painter, seizing his
Focus, illuminated, and what
Are we, unilluminated? What,
To go on, is illumination
For? In the painting, for instance,
The atrocity is not in fact
Visible on the streets but in the eyes
Of the painter—St. Luke. The painter,
Gazing only on the bright infant,
Instead of out the window, reaches
A conclusion not plainly implied
In infant glee. Yet St. Luke's face is plainly
Illuminated by what he sees
Directly before him, while I look
Over Roger's shoulder and out the
Window. And weep, to see the city
So delicate and outside, though
I grant the mistake, the mistake of
Weeping, that is, when perhaps I could
Move subtly into the paint and stand
Behind St. Luke. He looks calm enough.

But I, seeing what he sees, would have
No thought of Fridays, or windows, or

Outsides of any sort; this is
The essential weakness of eyes like

Mine, to see, faced with a divine light,
Nothing but divine light, which is why
Landscapes, or whatever you paint
Beyond the garden, become so central,
Not to the conception, which is all
Complete in what the saint sees, but
To the training of the eye that is,
After all, an action of painting

And illuminations. There are those
That descend to the street while the bright
Neon sign above the square that says
True Cigarets glows undiminished
As the hosts of heaven. In Boston,
Standing before this painting I thought,
Even as I was transported, of
Streets in general, the subway ride home,
And the expanse of walks, all crowded,
That lay between you and me at that
Moment. I thought, in short, of you. We

Have Roger to thank for this. With just
The Infant before me I might have
Stepped out of all those streets directly
Into the light—only in my mind,
Of course, thus forgetting the way

Home. As it was I found my way through
The shadows and arrived in your arms
Only slightly bruised, and all because
Roger kindly refrained from making
A portrait of Christ in unrelieved
Brilliance. Light is light. We are guided,
Sometimes, more easily by the faint
Revelations in the shapes shadows
Suggest than by the blank expanses
On the faces of stars. I find some
Guidance, anyway, in my dark fears
Of what lurks in the streets and come to
See the light more clearly because I

Have missed it so many times, many
Hours. Gaze at the ground, then look up,
Is my advice, and see the light, at last,
As precious because we find it
In the darkness outside a garden
Between the light and the world.

❧ Notes ❧

These are Vicki Hearne's explanatory notes, gathered here both from the manuscript of the unpublished poems and from the pages of the published poems (where they were given as footnotes). Those added by the editor are identified as [JH].

Page 10, Preliminary Note

In the final manuscript, Hearne had indicated that "this is preliminary to the poem 'Tricks of the Light' but could, I suppose, without incoherence usher in the whole volume." [JH]

Posthumous Poems

Page 17, "Some Exactitudes of Wonder from an Old Quest Manual":

Argos, Odysseus's hound, is the first one given to us by the full power of the imagination. And the first hound's name is "light" according to the Greek lexicon: *argos* means shining, or glistening, and in the form *argoi* referred to hounds and means literally "shining footed," which, in turn is understood to mean swift-footed because "in hounds all swift motion causes a kind of glancing or flickering lightly." (The lexicon suggests that the reader look up the Sanskrit for shining or swift. The association of the feet of swift hounds with light was not a passing fancy.)

Argos, like Odysseus, was mortal, but Homer gives us, in his description of the two sculpted hounds who guard the entrance to Alkinoös's house, shining and undying hounds "that never could grow old." Later, the poet tells us that Odysseus's hound, who was as keen on scent, as fleet and as brave and unconquerable as a hound can be, is named light. When Homer gives the name "Light" to the hound Argos, the immortal light of the golden and silver hounds of Alkinoös's house is reflected, not only in Argos's name, but in his very being, with every fleet move he makes.

Argos reflects immortality so well that, even dying, he seems to dazzle his master. Both were the stuff of nobility. Hence, neither acknowledged, for anyone's eyes but each other's, the meaning of the last minutes of the hound's life—

minutes that are in large part occupied with a recital of his greatness as a hunter, in an unbearably ironic setting, a gem come home by way of a life.

Page 38, "Upon Hearing That Helen Keller Has a Bull Pup": I had no textual authority for recasting the first six lines into three couplets—the meter of the whole poem—but it should probably be read that way. *With-/out comment* in manuscript (no hyphen). [JH]

Page 44, "A Subtle Gesture": last line, *at last, at rest;* other manuscript, *at last, in flight.* Comma deleted. [JH]

Page 46, "Delight in a Seasonal Shift": this poem was published in *Denver Quarterly* under the title "Syntax: Its Seasonal Shift." Fourth stanza, first line: *in fall;* earlier manuscript, *in spring.* [JH]

Page 47, "Trained Man and Dog": Second stanza, line eleven: *landscapes:;* in manuscript, *landscapes.* [JH]

Page 49, "So There Is Justice," Part I: I've left the anomalous indentation in the first two tercets, although they are most probably the result of uncorrected ellipses. [JH]

Page 52, "Young Dog, Grass, and More": changed stanza two line two to *For who will;* manuscript gives *For whom will.* [JH]

Tricks of the Light

Part I, first stanza: *That year;* in manuscript, *that year.* Thirteen lines later: *edge of that idea;* in manuscript, *edge that idea.* In the first fifty-eight lines of Part I, the versification exhibits arbitrary anomalies that disappear thereafter in all three parts of this long poem. They may be read as intentionally tentative-seeming approaches to the poem's standard meter—shorter free-verse tercets—but the general condition of the manuscript leads me to believe them to result from unintended accidents of formatting and residues of first-draft indecision. Page 62, line twenty-nine: the single line *and gold* is an apparently pointless anomaly, but in this case, I feel, functional. Nine lines later: *and swift;* in manuscript, *an swift.* [JH]

Part II, stanza seven: *dazzling . . . law.* In manuscript, this tercet is indented stepwise downward. Here and on page 69, in the tercet beginning *of wings,* I have adjusted the lineation. [JH]

Part III, stanza twelve: *love* was not italicized in the manuscript. In stanza eighteen: *You;* manuscript gives *Your.* Eight stanzas later: hyphen added to *overly-*

precise. Stanza thirty-seven: *neoteny; neotony* in manuscript. Neoteny is the reten-
tion of juvenile characteristics in a mature creature. [JH]

Part V, stanza twenty-two: *The sheepdog, see . . . drive* in manuscript is probably
a typo, either for *see [him / on . . . drive* (the comma supports this), or *seen,* or,
less likely, *sees,* or, with the comma moved to after *see,* an archaistic inver-
sion. [JH]

from *Nervous Horses*

Page 99, "Glitter: A Critical Essay": In manuscript Hearne had rewritten the
printed text as follows: *The evil men do gets after them* became *The evil I do gets after
me* and, subsequently throughout the poem, *our* was changed to *my.* The last
tercet of the poem became *Foolish poet, but by the very / Davar that comes to me
rightly / Radiant, ever gently, and pure.* The Hebrew word *Davar* means "word" or
"speech," but also "matter" or "something." [JH]

Page 102, "Rebreaking Outlaw Horses in the Desert": *"Depend / Upon it . . .
mare!"* Cox, trainer-groom for Sir Charles Dunbury, was dying in the spring of
1801. A few weeks later, Eleanor became the first filly to win both the Derby
and the Oaks.

Page 104, "Daedalus Broods on the Equestrian Olympic Trials": *Prix des Nations.*
The reader is asked to imagine that Daedalus is talking about a modern Grand
Prix jumping competition. Our sleep, Thus: one . . . two . . . three . . . Go! / At
Go, throw your heart over the fence. Hearne's handwritten note here read (OR
one . . . two, one one . . . OR get out now!) . . . because / They are familiar was
changed to because / Somewhat familiar. [JH]

Page 110, "Emergence": *epiphanal.* Hearne's nonce usage (like Charles Lamb's
"epiphanous" for the usual "epiphanic." (See also "The Singing Lesson," p. 116.)

Page 113, "Waking": Epigraph: Gulley Jimson is the painter-hero of Joyce Cary's
The Horse's Mouth (1944). *stupid questing* corrected in the manuscript to *hide-
bound questing.* [JH]

Page 117, "A Photograph" (a note on the dedication): In this case, "thoroughbred-
Arabian" means "purebred Arabian". It does not mean "Anglo-arab," that is, it
does not refer to a cross between an Arabian and a Thoroughbred.

Page 122, "Science and Human Behavior": The title is that of the behaviorist
psychologist B. F. Skinner's (1904–90) book of 1953. [JH]

Page 126, "My Father Rode Great, Silver Birds": similarly a correction made to
the printed volume's text, where it reads Parakeets who not only flew, . . . Sang,
and one of them even talked was corrected to Parakeets who flew, // Flashing
multicolored, but also / Sang. The Very best of them talked. [JH]

from *In the Absence of Horses*

Page 137, "Ana Halach Dodeach": *Title:* "Wither is thy beloved gone?" Song of
Solomon, 6.1. [JH]

Page 146, "The Claim of Speech": The title here alludes to that of the philosopher
Stanley Cavell's important book *The Claim of Reason: Wittgenstein, Skepticism,
Morality, and Tragedy* (1979). [JH]

Page 147, "On R. L. S. and Happiness": *Title:* Robert Louis Stevenson? [JH]

Page 163, "Gauguin's White Horse": Paul Gauguin, *Le Cheval Blanc,* 1889, Musée
d'Orsay, Paris. [JH]

Page 166, "Ierushalayim Shel Zahav": *Title:* "Jerusalem of Gold." It is the title
of a popular Israeli song, very lyrical and tender, which the Israeli soldiers sang
in 1967 when they took over the Old City; "thirty Jews" refers to the sometime
tradition that there are thirty good men in the world, and the world will cease to
exist if any of them should cease to be good.

from *The Parts of Light*

The ordering of the poems in this section, unlike that of Hearne's selections
from the two previous books, is not as they appeared in the original publication.
Hearne rearranged them in the way given here, which allowed her to end the
book with the very fine poem on the Roger van der Weyden painting. [JH]

Page 176, "Some General Principles of the Art of Riding": *Mary Chapot,* the first
female show-jumping rider to win a gold at the Pan Am Games, rode a horse
named White Lighting to a victory in Winnipeg in 1967. *D'Endrody:* Lt. Col. A. L.
d'Endrody was a celebrated equestrian trainer and author of *Give Your Horse A
Chance: A Classic Work on the Training of Horse and Rider* (1959). *Grisone:* Federico
Grisone set up an equestrian school in 1532 in Italy and was the author of the
widely translated *Gli ordini di cavalcare (The Rules of Horsemanship)* (1550). *Pessoa:*
Nelson Pessoa Filho, a Brazilian show-jumper who rode Gran Geste to a win in
Dublin in 1963. *Steinkraus:* William C. Steinkraus was an American Olympic gold
medalist and author of several books on the subject of horsemanship. [JH]

Page 180, "Girl on a Lawn": *mongoloid* as a word has only recently come to be regarded as an offensive characterization of a person with Down's syndrome. [JH]

Page 194, "Before the War": *sheepdog . . . shepherds:* the sheepdog of line 3 is a herding dog; Job's dogs were almost without a doubt a flock-guarding breed. *Socrates . . . pity:* In Book II of the *Republic,* Socrates says that an eye must be kept on the poets, for some of them have it that the gods are unkind to each other. The phrase *the lion . . . gate:* When the Israelis took over the Old City in 1967, they entered at the place (gate) called The Lion's Gate.

Page 197, "St. Luke Painting the Virgin": Roger van der Weyden's painting, otherwise known as the St. Luke Madonna, c. 1435–1440, is in The Museum of Fine Arts, Boston. [JH]

A Note on the Editing

The manuscript of the long title poem presented the most editorial difficulties of all the ones Hearne had assembled by the time of her death. Punctuation and capitalization—as in some of the other poems—needed editorial attention, but there were also occasional ellipses, a few spots of momentary incoherence, and, particularly, of erratic lineation. These are all changes that Hearne licensed me to make, and the printed text of the poem depends largely on the suggestions made to me by Stewart. The metrical norm of "Tricks of the Light" is that of the open, heavily enjambed short free-verse lines, arranged in tercets, and formatted flush left, in which so many of the other poems were cast. There are occasional isolated single lines (felt and, I believe, intended, as a pacing device within what are frequently very long periodic sentences); on the other hand, there are some anomalous indentations. But the early pages are inconsistently and dysfunctionally versified; in the interests of greater accessibility to this otherwise fruitfully problematic work, I have made a number of changes for the printed text. With the exception of changes in punctuation, they are given in the "Notes" section above, along with a few changes in the poems from "Posthumous Poems" that were made prior to periodical publication.

Index of Titles and First Lines